Messing
about in Boats

The Nautical Confessions
of an Unsinkable Irishman

Messing
about in Boats

The Nautical Confessions
of an Unsinkable Irishman

Will Millar

formerly of
the *Irish Rovers*

Whitecap Books

Vancouver/Toronto

The information in this book is true and complete to the best of our knowledge. All recommendations are made without guarantee on the part of the author or Whitecap Books Ltd. The author and publisher disclaim any liability in connection with the use of this information. For additional information please contact Whitecap Books Ltd., 351 Lynn Avenue, North Vancouver, BC, V7J 2C4.

For permission to reproduce the poem "Sea Fever" on page 32, the author acknowledges The Society of Authors as the Literary Representative of the Estate of John Masefield.

Edited by Carolyn Bateman
Proofread by Elizabeth McLean
Cover photograph by Jim Morrison
Interior design and typeset by Warren Clark

Printed and bound in Canada.

Canadian Cataloguing in Publication Data

Millar, Will 1939–
    Messing about in boats

    ISBN 1-55110-620-5
    1. Millar, Will, 1939– 2. Boats and boating—Anecdotes.
3. Boats and boating—Humor. I. Title
GV777.3.M54 1997   797.1'0207   C97-910660-5

We acknowledge the support of the Canada Council for the Arts for our publishing program and the Cultural Services Branch of the Government of British Columbia in making this publication possible.

For more information on other titles from Whitecap Books, visit our web site at www.whitecap.ca

To the salty old sea dogs who sailed me along
And all the sweet sirens who sang me their song
To the man on the squeezebox who gave me a tune
On our fine sailing trips that were over too soon
To the blue-eyed madonna from the high western land
Who gave me small pirates to hold by the hand
To all of the ones who came for to sing
And share in the chorus and make rafters ring
To the friends who believed I could handle the sail
And helped me to laugh in the teeth of the gale

Contents

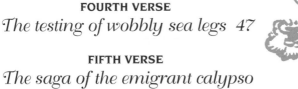

The song of the Irish Rover

One wintery day in the spring of the year
We sailed out from the fair Cove of Cork.
We were bound far away with a cargo of clay
For a grand City Hall in New York.
Our ship was a craft that was built in Belfast
And many's the wild wind rolled her.
We had canvas by the mile and we sailed away in style
On the ship called the *Irish Rover*.

Chorus: So fare thee well my own true love, I am going far
    away,
And I will swear by the stars above forever I'll be true.
But as we part it breaks my heart and when this trip is
    o-o-over
I'll sail back in style, in true Irish style,
On the ship called the *Irish Rover*.

We were five years from shore when the whiskey ran dry
And the mate Mick McGee lost his head.
Big Pat McCann from the banks of the Bann
Cursed and swore, wished to God he was dead,
So our captain checked the charts (he knew every pub by
    heart)
And we stopped at them all coming over.
Then whiskey kegs galore, ten thousand maybe more,
Were loaded on the *Irish Rover*.

We had one million bags of the best Sligo rags,
We had two million barrels of stone,
Three million sides of old blind horses' hides,
We had four million barrels of bone,
Five million hogs, and six million dogs,
We had seven million barrels of porter,
We had eight million bales of old nanny goat tails
On board of the *Irish Rover*.

There was old Mickey Coote who played hard on his flute
When the ladies lined up for a "set."
He could tootle with skill, they stepped out with a will,
He could play all night long you can bet.
With his smart witty talk he was "Cock of the Walk"
As he "rowled" the girls under and over.
When he took his stance they all knew at a glance
That he sailed on the *Irish Rover*.

For a sailor it's always a bothering life,
It's so lonesome by night and by day,
And ye'll long for the shore and a charming young . . .
   wife
Who will melt all yer troubles away.
All the gales and the wrecks, pouring poteen down yer
   neck,
This life ye'd soon give o-o-over,
With a wife on the shore I'm sure you'll never more
Go to sea on the *Irish Rover*.

I'm the last of the pirates, those "buckos" so tough,
An old salt who has weathered the storm.
Be the breezes asleep, or the sea wild and rough,
We were always in top fighting form!
For we were the boys who had tasted life's joys,
On shore we were all in clover,
For women, wine, and song lasted all the years along
For the lads of the *Irish Rover*.

Well we sailed thirty years when some madness hit
    the crew
And our ship hit a rock in the fog,
Then the whole of the crew was reduced down to two,
Just myself and the captain's old dog.
Then the ship struck a rock, O Lord what a shock!
The *Rover* she turned right o-o-over,
Turned nine times around and the poor oul dog was
    drowned . . .
I'm the last of the *Irish Rover*.

This is my vision of the Irish Rover

Before we weigh anchor and set sail

*M*ore than a hundred years ago, some old sailor scratched the beginnings of this Irish ballad to amuse his shipmates on some hard voyage to distant, foreign shores. The song was picked up by the droves of hungry emigrant musicians and singers, where it made its way onto the stages of Boston and New York, and into the vaudeville houses of Toronto and Sydney. It is probably one of the best-known Irish street ballads or stage Irish songs of them all.

That song became a big part of my life, and this story is about a voyage on that wildly reckless and rambunctious vessel. My sailings aboard her were often haphazard and downright dangerous; they were also hilarious and joyful— even rewarding—with just a drop of nostalgia and melancholy to keep this Celtic navigator from losing sight of the fact that life is a short voyage.

Across all the years of my life I have considered myself a sailor first and foremost, and the boats in this story are all real or at least were real while they were afloat. When you read my log you can judge for yourself just what caliber of seaman I turned out to be. I promise that I will tell you most of the important log entries in my odyssey to these current shores.

I am glad to say that I found some healthy success as leader of the Irish Rovers—a singing group of some renown, which counted thirty-five records and at least two worldwide hits as trophies of that thirty-year voyage. The *Irish Rover* may never have been a real ship, but by God it was a genuine tall music ship that carried me across the world a few times. I sang out that lusty chantey chorus everywhere from the Sydney Opera House to Carnegie Hall in New York and hundreds of small towns and seaports in between. The crowds would join the chorus, and they came year after year to hear me and my rebellious crew roar out once more, "I'm the last of the *Irish Rover.*"

I was born to the sea and music was my nursemaid. The melody of my father's little squeezebox lilted a sea song for me since the day I first saw those Antrim cliffs in the short winter light. The north coast of Ireland was a magic kingdom where a boy with my imagination could grow to be a dreamer. Ruined castles were built on the remains of older forts, and crumbling stone ramparts echoed the blood-curdling war cries of Viking warriors as their longships sliced through the mists of the north.

Just off the beaches, where we rode little summer donkeys, were Spanish galleons sunk since the time of the great Armada. There they waited, in the cold green depths, to be discovered. It was in these surroundings that I learned my love for Irish music. I also acquired my often near-fatal attraction for that wild ocean and the tiny, fragile craft in which human beings somehow manage, most of the time, to keep afloat. I was called to that mightiest of all of God's creations from the very start.

My world was small in that Irish town and foreign places

intrigued me. As a young boy I collected postage stamps, and all those colorful little pictures with strange-sounding names like Sierra Leone, Madagascar, Ivory Coast, and Tahiti sent some kind of thrill through my restless young spirit. Boats seemed to me to be the magic carpet that could take me to the world of my stamps.

I loved the look of sailing boats and the freedom they promised. Yet King Neptune, that mythological old ruler of the deep and all things that dare to sail upon his waters, must have taken a dislike to me even as a minnow. His pointy trident has prodded my arse on a number of occasions. He has hurled hailstones and hurricanes at my fragile hull often enough, and though he battered and beat me manys a time, I'm still afloat to tell the tale. I like to imagine that deep in the depths of his indigo heart he admires the Irish luck that helped me survive quite a few rounds with the old sovereign of the seas.

I am sure he knows that just beneath the surface of civilized thinking, I preserve a reverent pagan place for his vast untamed seascapes. With my Celtic chants rending the air, I made many attempts to sacrifice vessels to him and I believe he tolerates me for that at least. More than once I've heard him bellow his encouragement to me in the wild winds.

Beyond the misty horizon his sirens call to the Saint Brendan the Navigator in me. That old Irish monk set sail, they say, on a boat made of willow branches and ox hides. He had the audacity to sail to America sometime in the fourth century—long before the Italian fellow in 1492. The Irish are a seafaring race and I am soaked (many times over) in our natural need to be near or upon the ocean. Each and every floating thing that ever I climbed aboard transformed this dryland sailor into a salty swashbuckler.

As a child I graduated in the fine art of profanity at

Neptune's watery college of rotted wood and rusted marine machinery. My professors were a rum-soaked crew of shipwrights, whalers, gill-netters, lobstermen, and deep-sea sailors—gentlemen all from every compass point. Even today, whenever I'm within five miles of a body of water, my everyday conversation becomes peppered with silly nautical terms, half of them most likely misused. (It took me the longest time to distinguish starboard and that other side.) Nevertheless, I always believed I had the makings of a first-class skipper ready to lose that bloody albatross.

One of the first books I received from my hardworking mother was Kenneth Grahame's classic *The Wind in the Willows*. There is a fine motto in that story for anyone who complains about the problems and the cost of maintaining a sailboat. I see it as the perfect nautical reminder to paint on every bulkhead. Rat is introducing Mole to the wee blue rowboat: "Believe me, my young friend," he says, "there is *nothing*—absolutely nothing—half so much worth doing as simply messing about in boats . . ."

I wholeheartedly agreed! I spent my boyhood around the sea corners of Northern Ireland, with its many little harbors and colorful wooden boats. My dreams of being a sailor were fired by books like Robert Louis Stevenson's *Treasure Island*. Jim Hawkins, the cabin boy–adventurer, seemed to be just my age, and I sailed on many joyful mind voyages as "Jim" aboard a treasure-seeking ship, with Long John and his mutinous crew.

Climb aboard the *Irish Rover* with me and I will tie a few knots in the yarn of my nautical confessions. I will travel with you from that coastal boyhood in Ireland to many ports of adventure, where danger, recklessness, and sheer good luck and sailing fun are part of the ship's log. You may glean some nautical wisdom from the many old salts who crossed my path. You may laugh or cry at some of the fates that seemed to

lie in wait for me every time I dared to go near the water.
Perhaps you may pick up a bit of nautical nonsense or
discover some more about boats and why we love them and
hate them so much. Or maybe you'll just learn to be careful
when someone like me invites you for a day's sailing.

The timber is seasoned for the keel of the Irish Rover

*T*he first time I sang that song about the Irish Rover was at a talent contest in the seaside town of Portrush when I was eleven. It was short tweedy trousers in those days and knee-socks forever falling over boot tops. The weather seemed to be always drizzling during those singing summers as my Da played along on the little accordion. Some of the crowd came in to hear us, the others came in to get out of the wet. Trailing mud and water from their sea boots, they would wander into the Portrush town hall. They clapped and booed, raged and sang. They cheered, crunched fish and chips and bags of seaweed called "dulse" and sucked something sweet and brownish-yellow called Yella Man. "Come on," I'd yell from the stage in my piping boy-soprano voice. "Everybody sing, 'I'm the last of the Irish Rover.'" I got a good part of my education from this motley crew.

My mother's father dabbled now and then in real estate. He would let us live rent-free in his old houses around the town of Ballymena, County Antrim, in exchange for fixing them up. After my parents had improved the house, it would be sold at a modest profit. Then like gipsies we would pack up our meager belongings and shift to the next fix-em-upper. This probably explains my dream of living on a boat, for I believed that when it was time to move on a boat, your home could travel with you. Luckily my Irish world was small, and our big moves were only to a different street, so I attended the same school most of the time and plundered the town with my same playmates.

There was a period of almost two years when my grandfather had no house deal pending for us. We had to travel thirty miles to the sea coast and the beautiful town of Portrush, where Uncle Joe let us live in one of his rental caravans. Of course when I heard the news I was jumping up and down with glee at the chance to live at the seaside. Since winter was around the corner, my mother was less than enthusiastic at the thought of hauling her family to a rickety dwelling on the bleak cliffs overlooking the sea. I was around eleven and ready for any adventure or change that came along.

The leaky tin-roofed caravan was perched on the long grass slopes of the ocean-sprayed cliffs, just outside the town. It was not a real caravan for it had been converted into a bungalow from the carriage of an old train. At one end my mother and father had a little room behind a curtain. At the opposite side, the three children shared a two-tier bunk bed. Since I was the oldest, I commandeered the top bunk with the little porthole looking out to sea. The two younger children used the bottom, in a mad orgy of fighting and Irish rebellion.

The battered railway carriage had a little name sign on the door that read "Lower Lights Cottage." I think my mother got the line from an old Scottish mariner's hymn called "Let the Lower Lights Be Burning." It always reminded me of a notice warning people to "dip" their lights.

My mother, bless her heart, had come from a religious farm family. I am sure she had never expected to be living so far from her father's land in a ramshackle caravan with a musician and three scrapping children. Her hopes of a cozy town house with a nice little "Devon grate" fireplace had flown away again because of my father's difficulty in finding work. On threadbare wings those soaring hopes had flapped, once more unable to stay aloft. All she could do was depend on her father's next real estate deal.

Our new seaside abode was without plumbing, so we were forced to carry fresh water from a pump half a mile away, and dump a heavy, splashing bucket of not-so-fresh contents over the cliffs and down into the forgiving sea. I'm sure there was manys an early morning fisherman below those cliffs who must have been surprised by the texture of the rain.

The caravan faced the wild Atlantic and we were often rocked by the wild north wind. The windows were spotted with dried salt spray and the gray clouds blanketed us in those long winter days. I would lie cozily in the small top bunk, listening to the ocean roar. Drifting off to sleep, I would count the

Me Da on the squeezebox

constant hiss of raindrops dripping through the ceiling onto the red-hot lid of the old iron stove. The airy lilt and cry of my father's accordion music soaked into the room sometimes from the cottage next door where he spent a lot of time playing cards with some of his cronies. Now and then, when the drink would trigger the muse, he would entertain the company with a few "oul tunes."

The top bunk became my berth at sea, and it was easy to pretend that the button-key accordion sound was now an old concertina, played by the man in the fo'c's'le of my good ship *Irish Rover*. When the wind whistled up the wild heather hillsides around the caravan, I would curl deeper into my worn flannel sheets and old knitted woolen quilts. Under my blanket sky I reveled in the booming sea and the swirling gulls who cried their joy to the north wind. I was on a voyage then with the characters in my books, off to places only dreamers can hope to find.

It was that stamp collection of mine and also my books that first fed the desire in me to be sailing. Without radio and certainly without television, I read books about the sea and exotic places far beyond Ireland. I hated to come to the end of the story. That restless gipsy spirit in my soul stirred in me early. Oh, how I longed for a glimpse of aquamarine lagoons and palms. I would wheeze with asthma in that coal smoke air and dream of warm winds and parrots on islands of coconuts and banana trees. I would tell my little sister and brother, "Someday I am going to sail you all to a place where the air is 'fragrant with sweet flowers.'" (I often quoted to them from the books.)

"Will there be cowboys there?" asked my little brother; "and drum majorettes?" chimed in my hopeful sister, who was caught up in America and had taken to wrecking our present house with her whirling and mostly out-of-control homemade baton, accompanied by brass band music from an old windup gramophone. Both my younger siblings somehow escaped my lemming course to the sea.

I always think of it as a happy childhood. Most of my memories are full of pleasant snapshots of nostalgia that can still bring joy to my mind. I can see myself sitting on the high cliffs watching the rolling waves below and scanning the far-off western horizon with longing. I can still experience a youthful shudder when I think of the power of the great surges as the swells rushed over the dark rocks. The mighty fanfare of breaking surf hurled sea foam and spray all the way up the cliffs to soak my face. I wanted to clear past the breakers and the frothing rocks, feel the sea under the deck, and head away from the land.

To this day, when I stand by the sea and look toward the horizon there comes that longing to be under sail. Canvas unfurling in the freshening breeze brings a pang in my heart to be leaving. No matter what contented shore space I luckily fall into, before long there will be a gull's cry and my mind will hear the chantey chorus one more time. The sail will billow, the ship shudders with anticipation, and I'm bows-under heading south to sunny islands pictured in that colorful old stamp collection.

I cannot pinpoint exactly where I first earned my notoriety as a jinxed deck hand, but somehow things seemed to go wrong whenever I came near a boat. My misadventures have fallen into folklore by the people who know me. I just laugh and shrug, and have fantasies about sailing them all through wild storms, emerging into the calm where they are eternally grateful that I was such an experienced skipper.

I grew up hearing the story of one of my first nautical mishaps, told and retold by my family—particularly my mother and her confidante, her sister Sadie. Those two women loved to laugh together, with great irreverence too, at any unfortunate soul they considered a fool. They fed each other line after line of some well-used saga of a humorous event, and then they would fall into fits of uncontrollable gaiety. It was a truly infectious madness as they rolled about in great peals of joyful laughter.

Their brother, my poor old Uncle Joe, was the subject of many a wild comedy fest. One story that was particularly well repeated concerned Joe and his new bride and how I almost killed him in a rowboat . . . on his wedding day to boot! Joe, who was not a handsome individual, had waited until he was forty before he thought about getting married. He never paid much attention to oral hygiene and a couple of large brown front teeth were all that showed when he smiled. To top off his idea of being handsome he developed a wire-brush hairdo, which he constantly slicked down with gobs of Brylcreem. His twitchy eyebrows gave him a surprised look; they were long and bushy and met in the middle, and they made him look like a villain in a silent movie. I always wished I could have combed them smooth with Brylcreem as well.

He constantly wore a blue serge suit that looked well slept in and his once-white shirt with the collar tips chewed away was decorated with an oily and colorful tie. He sported a pair of rubber boots that he made shiny by painting them with black enamel. They were worn with the trousers tucked in, which kept them from getting caught in the chain of his bicycle. For all his eccentricities, he was a good-hearted and generous soul. Half the town of Ballymena owed him money for his cheap furniture, which he bought in auctions and resold on the buy-now-pay-never Irish plan.

He had saved a modest sum of money so there were those girls who felt that as they had almost "passed their market," he might be a good catch. He finally found himself a fine strapping one at a Young Farmers Society dance. Bridget O'Looney was her name and she stood six feet tall in her stocking feet and had a big red happy face, the kind of woman that the farmers would say "wasn't bullied at the trough." After watching her all evening at the dance, he finally got the nerve up to ask her for a dance. As they executed the fox trot across the floor, he whispered breathless to her, "Can I have the last dance with you?" She looked down at him and answered with a great braying laugh, "Yer havin' it!"

After a couple of weeks of heavy courting he asked her to marry him. "How would you like to be buried with my people?" was his passionate proposal. The big girl thought this very romantic and promptly agreed. Romantic or not, it was a grand wedding all the same. I was about eight at the time, and my Uncle Archie, who was a tailor, made me a pair of long trousers out of an old pair of his own. "My first long trousers," I announced rather dramatically to a young cousin who stared at them in envy.

I remember the men made a fuss of me by standing me up on a bar table for all the pub crowd to see. "Give us a song, son," they called out. After I had completed all seven verses of "The Irish Rover," my party piece, they slipped a few shillings into my new pockets and clapped me on my skinny little back, as though I had just passed some secret male ritual and emerged as a fully fledged hunter and sailor in my long pants. I can tell you I was very excited about the whole thing and couldn't stop admiring my new adult-looking legs reflected in the shop windows.

This would be my first time attending a wedding and they said that there would be a real feast with lots of currant cake and tinned fruit. I had never tasted tinned fruit before so I was ready. Best of all, we were going boating in Joe's rowboat, one he had acquired in yet another junk-trading expedition. I had been helping to get it ready for the big day and I liked the look of that boat. Even though it was a bit punky here and there, it had a graceful line, with its planking painted blue and white.

The wedding day dawned bright and clear. We threw colored paper and dried peas (since we had no rice) at the couple as they left the church. A fiddler rattled out the Scottish reel "Off to Marie's Wedding," and everybody sang:

> *Step we gaily on we go*
> *Heel for heel and toe for toe.*
> *Arm in arm and row on row*
> *All for Marie's Wedding.*

There was a noisy guest list of uncles and aunts, and some had traveled from as far as Donegal to join the merry throng. There were young men in old suits and old women with new handbags. Ragamuffin children played wild games around the church graveyard. Two Teddy boys with slicked-down hair and cigarettes dangling from their mouths in the style of Humphrey Bogart played pitch and toss on top of the big flat gravestones. The minister spotted their sin and rushed over with the fire of our vengeful Lord, crying, "Money changers and gam-bo-leers!" He scattered the coins, took the spoils for the poor box, and damned their souls to hell at the same time for good measure.

Everyone went mad on the feast at the old guest house where my mother worked. There was a great Irish cacophony of sound as the soup was slurped and the beef was bolted down with pints of Guinness and cheap wine. After a great feed we all headed out to enjoy the summery sea air at the harbor and take some photographs. My grannies and granda and tipsy uncles rolled their clothes up above their knees to paddle in the sea and tied knots in the corners of their white handkerchiefs, wearing these hanky hats to save them from the pale Irish sun. One uncle went harvesting limpets off rocks with a little penknife. He swallowed them raw, telling everyone how healthy they were for the body, and how we should "get stuck into a feed!" Later, after a few more pints of the black porter and a couple or three Bushmills whiskeys, he was strung across the rocks, as green as the seaweed, and uttering unearthly noises, wishing himself dead.

I strutted in my new manhood in long pants, across the harbor wall just above where Joe and his new bride were preparing to take the first row. I waved gaily to them and insisted to my Da that I should get to cast the rope that was holding them to the dock. Joe, pointing up to the dock, yelled to my Da, "Lower that wee anchor down to me." In my anxiety to be the sole deck hand for this voyage, I rushed over and picked up the wrong anchor. The one I grabbed was much bigger and altogether too heavy for me. I struggled over to the edge of the wall. "NO!" yelled my Da. "No! Drop it!" So I did, but instead of lowering it to Joe in the boat below, I let it slip through my hands with a burning screech! The old rusted anchor hurtled down fifteen feet, narrowly missing the top of Joe's new bowler hat. It opened up a plank in the bottom of the antique rowboat with a mighty crack. Joe's new bride jumped up and her weight upset the round-bottomed tub, toppling her into the cold harbor in her going-away suit.

Bridget was screaming and floundering and trying to hold on to the side of the rocking rowboat. Then Joe, with a good show of derring-do, carefully removed his wedding bowler hat and set it on the seat of the boat. Next came his new coat, with the big spray of flowers. Stripped for action to his suspenders, he leaped out into the chilly water, forgetting he couldn't swim. The din was terrific and people were running up and down the dock. Someone threw a rope into the boat, but unfortunately it was not attached to anything. Bridget grabbed an end of it anyway, and there she was back in the water holding a thirty-foot length of rope.

After she got over the chill and the shock of the dunking, she took control. Uncle Joe felt her stout farmer's arms around him and she managed to float the both of them over to the iron ladder, where three or four hefty men pulled them out. A few dry coats were offered, and the newlyweds were rushed back to the welcoming fireside in the guest house. The whole wedding company trooped back into the bar, and the music and the joking commenced once more. Joe and his bride crept up the stairs to their wedding bed armed with a couple of hot whiskeys.

After I let the anchor go that started this chain reaction of exotic water sports, I skulked off in horror and hid out in a shed until I saw all the merrymakers heading back to the pub. When they were all inside, I crept out and peered in the steamy window of the lighted room. Then, satisfied that they were not going to lynch me or send me off to a Borstal school for wayward boys, I hurried back to the scene of the crime. The rowboat was now half full of water and would soon be lying on the bottom of the harbor. I asked Dan Hannoway, an old fisherman, to help me save "my" boat. We hauled and pulled away at the unwieldy load of water until we had her safely upside down on the stone steps.

The old fellow asked me if I would like a drink of Guinness. I was thinking that he was probably deceived by my long pants, taking me for a small adult. I told him in my best macho voice that I was "off the stuff." He nodded and admitted that he too was trying to give it up. As he downed the last of his bottle he told me to come around some time and he would show me how to caulk and repair the old boat.

I am glad that my family knew that laughter was the best

cure for a lot of the woes that life can dish out. Even through
the slim times, when we were hard pressed to come up with
the basics of life, there were always old songs and stories full
of laughter to brighten the day. I remember, when Uncle Joe
was ill in the last few weeks of his life, how he laughed heartily
with me about the boat, and Bridget in the harbor on his
wedding day, and about the time that his little rowboat
introduced me to one of my first terrors of the deep.

Sea fever

As I let my thoughts journey back along the waterways of my life, Uncle Joe's old wooden rowboat
leads a flotilla of vessels that comes gurgling along
to pass under the bridge that connects my reason to
John Masefield's rhyme of "Sea Fever." I could recite the whole
poem by heart when I was ten for I was the boy to call on in
English class if you needed a colorful rendition of a sailor's
poem. Our teacher, the fearsome Mrs. Marshall, showed a
trace of leniency toward me because I could recite poetry with
passion.

She was a large, flowery woman who smelled of chalk, old
roses, and a vague aroma that reminded me of my granda's
Erinmore pipe tobacco. She took a shine to me, and I felt
lucky in that regard for some of my mates were terrified of
her temper tantrums.

Her whistling cane snapped across my dirty hands only
once or twice during my time with her, and I am certain my
good fortune was not due entirely to my behavior. I would
close my eyes as I stood in front of the class and feel every
passionate line of Mr. Masefield's:

I must go down to the seas again, to the lonely sea and the sky,
And all I ask is a tall ship and a star to steer her by,
And the wheel's kick and the wind's song and the white sail's shaking,
And a gray mist on the sea's face, and a gray dawn breaking.

I must go down to the seas again, for the call of the running tide
Is a wild call and a clear call that may not be denied;
And all I ask is a windy day with the white clouds flying,
And the flung spray and the blown spume, and the sea gulls crying.

I must go down to the seas again, to the vagrant gypsy life,
To the gull's way and the whale's way where the wind's like a whetted
     knife;
And all I ask is a merry yarn from a laughing fellow-rover
And quiet sleep and a sweet dream when the long trick's over.
                                        —"Sea Fever," John Masefield

My early school days were spent in the church school in the
town of Ballymena. It was a dark gray stone building that had
processed four generations of mill workers' children before I
was reluctantly dragged, yelling and kicking, through its
battered doors of learning.

I recently returned home to Ballymena for one of my
annual visits. The mayor presented me with a plaque of the
coat of arms of the town. As I stood in that old town hall to
receive the honor they bestow on exiles who have spread the
town's name around the world, I let my memory take me back
to my early days in the fifties, when the town was much less
prosperous. A huge shopping mall stands on the site of the
old Fair Hill markets. They are planning another mall on the
site of the mill, where my father and two generations before
him spent a hard part of their lives.

Ballymena in 1948 was a drab kind of town in those
days after the war, with a gasworks in the center spewing out

dirty yellow smoke. Not far from that hellish place was the Braidwater Mill, where a large number of townsfolk were employed. It was all Victorian brick with a tall chimney that could be seen from a long way off. The town had a coat of arms showing seven towers and this chimney somehow qualified as one of the seven.

I would often escape the gray and the smoke by wandering out to my mother's old home. Two miles beyond the grime lay a fairyland of green fields, hawthorn hedges, and ancient Celtic forts. A lazy green river streamed through that boyhood, winding over peat bogs and old forests. The same water that flowed dirty through the big mill sang clear and silent out there among the wildfowl. I fished from its banks, waded through the rocky shallows, and stared with awe at its deep dark pools.

I can well remember carving small sailboats out of branches, with leaves for sails and a tin soldier aboard to steer. Then I would follow along the bank as they bobbed, dipped, and finally disappeared around a bend in the river. My imagination had me aboard in place of the tin soldier, heading for the open sea. Over the years the image of that quiet spot has stayed with me.

It was a haunted place, and a vague memory comes to me of a small girl called Violet who drowned there one summer. Her father used to walk the mossy pathway for years afterward, under the roof of the spreading beech trees, handing out pamphlets etched with violet flowers and religious verse.

The place became my green flowing ribbon to the world. It was a tropical ocean, the Amazon River, and the White Nile all rolled into one. The gurgling ripples would grow and tumble over shining rocks as they joined the flood of other tea-brown bogland streams, rushing like me to the sea. That Irish stream infected me with a sea fever that would plague me all my life.

My first crew: Harry and George, with me on the right

School got in the way of my rambles when spring came with its swollen rivers and fragrant hawthorn blooms and primroses along their banks. Some days my friends and I missed going into school at all, hiding out in the park nearby, deeply engaged in the plans for our voyage of an Irish *Kon-Tiki*. There was never any problem finding excuses to remain in the fields by the rolling river long after the school bell sounded the end of dreaming.

Then joyful summer! We schemed the long days away in the quiet countryside outside the town. I had a place that I would go, a retreat, where the river gathered strength and rushed over the weirs anxious to join the sea. There we would stretch out among the long grass and chart our course to manhood and faraway places.

On the first week of that tenth summer of my growing, when the Irish countryside was most glorious, I got my first faint siren call to sailing adventure. Before long, my first *Irish Rover* vessel was taking shape in our backyard. The desire was so strong in me to float that deep, green river that I stole wood, rope, and some big biscuit tins from the back of Elliot's corner shop. After days of haphazard construction, I surveyed my strange raft. The first floating love of my life was born, not sleek and beautiful, but a thing of danger and excitement.

At that early age I had acquired some inflated and deluded bravery about the art of sailing. I remember a picture pinned on my wall, torn from an old *National Geographic*, that showed a strapping Yankee youth behind the wheel of a tall ship. In my boyhood daydreams I adopted that image for my own. There I was, a deep-sea sailor, robust and suntanned, at the helm of a great windjammer plowing round Cape Horn. The real me— that wheezy, white-legged, skinny boy—disappeared quite readily on my dreamscape ocean.

With a boating adventure burning a hole in my sailor's ambition and a vessel to explore the world, it was time to recruit a hardy crew. I have a little snapshot of "my men," showing me in my new long pants (looking the worse for wear since Uncle Joe's wedding). The other two are Harry Coulter, who was my first mate, and my younger brother, George, forever the reluctant and insecure shipmate. Harry, the red-headed adventurer, came from my street corner and together we plundered the 1950s. We managed to torment our long-suffering mothers without even trying.

Sunshine and warm winds heralded the launch day. I had not given any thought to the problem of transporting the raft to the river, which lay two miles away, but the ever scheming Harry brought an old pram from home. It was one of those English-style baby buggies, and we stripped the body off and kept the undercarriage. His mother was distraught when she found out; she kept things for nostalgia's sake, and I suppose the pram was a reminder of her babies. I tied an old door on top of the wheels, then with a good deal of push and shove we got the raft on top of the door.

Off we went, dragging the contraption behind us down the street. Neighbors thought we were collecting stuff for the annual bonfire. When we passed Mrs. O'Neill's house, she threw a couple of old tires from her backyard up on to the raft. Before we could object, someone added a broken chair to the pile of junk. They were fiercely loyalist around those street corners and the Twelfth of July bonfire was always a gala historic event.

Those two half-hearted shipmates helped me to wheel my *Kon-Tiki* all the way through town, and along the country road to the haunted river. There we launched it with a hearty splash and it settled at a tipsy angle, half afloat. "It floats! It floats! It bloody well floats!" I screamed, jumping up and down on the mushy bank. I leaped aboard, urging my landlubber crew to be quick about it. They were slow in responding and seemed happy enough to offer me the honor of a solo maiden voyage.

The craft had now settled a little lower in the river until my knees were underwater. Somehow I poled the submarine raft across to the other wide bank, bursting with enthusiasm at the near-floating success. My crew gave a half-hearted cheer and I assured them that I'd return and bring them aboard.

Unfortunately the biscuit-tin floats were gurgling and bubbling vigorously with water. I was left stranded on the raft, which by this time was resting on the muddy bottom in the shallows of the far bank. When one of the tin floats came loose and floated away on the current, I felt an ache of loss that was destined to touch me with a cold stab a few more times in the sea lanes of my future. My little crew was already waving good-bye and heading home to tea.

Wet and somewhat deflated, I faced a long walk of a couple of miles along the marshy river before I found a bridge and sloshed my soggy way home. Of course by the time I had made it back to the outskirts of town, I had painted a new picture of my first crossing. My soul was now full of a seaman's elation. I comforted myself with the knowledge that at least it had floated for a while.

That first summer on the deep river, the raft boat was refloated time after time. My mother's thin blankets were tied as sails and the flotation cans were made watertight. Then on a warm Irish summer afternoon, I drifted a mile or more along the rolling river in perfect solitude. Cows followed curiously along the bank, and a kingfisher perched for a moment on my mast. I was doomed at that moment to follow the wake of a whole flotilla of boats great and small for the rest of my life. I am not sure what the need was in me to conquer that deep green, but after all the years I still drift off now and then to that long ago river.

I let the memory of that broad summer river come to mind, and the thought is like a mantra for me. It is a place for beginnings and I think we all have a need for such a peaceful landing when we steer into troubled seas. A quiet backwater that we sail to now and then. When life seems too full of the struggle, it is good to wade in the shallows of a childhood river and remember with smiles and tears all the dear and happy times and the people we loved.

From these first raft launchings I acquired the strange trait that has shaped all my life's adventures: the less shipshape a soul or a ship the more it draws me to try to make it "float." It is like a challenge that sweeps over my thinking. I acquired this trait, I know, from my mother, Elizabeth Currie Alexander, the squeezebox gipsy's wife. She taught me compassion for weak things, she showed me the magical creations of nature, and she gave me a joy of the sea. She encouraged me to rise early to enjoy the day from the first peep of dawn. I remember her shedding a tear for a fallen blackbird I had hit with a stone from a catapult. I never killed any of God's creatures after that.

Near the end of her life she loved to reminisce with me about all the foolish adventures we both had stumbled across in our restlessness. I would see her knitting in the half light of sunset, within view of her beloved sea, refusing to turn on the electric lights until the last rays of the day had left the sky. I can still hear her singing her favorite hymn:

All things bright and beautiful,
All creatures great and small,
All things wise and wonderful,
The Lord God made them all.

She kept very little for herself and shared all she had with the world. I will be glad to have just a trace of her in me for the rest of my days.

Of course, back then, when I was ten years old, it was a more combative relationship that I had with my mother. Especially when I returned soaking wet and full of talk about a dangerous rafting adventure on the river of dark water where children were known to have drowned. By the time my eleventh birthday had rolled around she was packing up to move us out of one more of her father's rental homes. She told me in later years that she always hoped that somehow he would see fit to donate one of these cheap houses to her. Then she could do a real job of making a home for her kids. It never happened.

THIRD VERSE

Mill pond commandos

Boats were always there, floating around my childhood memories. Some of my earliest recollections
are of huge warships steaming past the coast of
North Antrim. These historic waters have seen ships of war all
too often. Although I was too young to remember much about
World War II, there is one vivid sea battle escapade in my diary
of troubled waters.

Even though everyone on our street was poor we were not
really aware of hard times and we were a happy lot of children.
Our toys were homemade
and our playgrounds were
the fields, the tree-lined
rivers, and the seaside.
Luxury vessels were a rare
sight around our snug
stone harbors. There were
very few of those fancy
floating homes—the
ones you see nowadays

Our gang

choking every marina in North America, the ones that never seem to sail away.

With the end of the war, people were able to travel the sea lanes of the Atlantic once more and every so often a foreign yacht would visit my childhood harbor. I would watch as it hove into view, racing with the tide into the narrow entrance. I loved the sight of canvas dropping and the rush of crew members working the sails and making ready for docking. There was always a longing in me to be part of that crew. A foreign flag slapping at the masthead always excited me. I would stand in awe as the sails came down at the last minute, just when I was sure there was no way they could stop before they rammed into the sea wall.

I would hang around the ships that had just crossed some mysterious ocean, watching the crew busy on deck. The sailors on board were not bound by dull mill work like my father and mother. They didn't have to face the tempers of possessed school masters who nailed me for my poor responses to math and science. Once in a while I would offer to run some errands for the ship's crew. That way I'd get to go aboard. I loved the smells and the sounds, the shiny brass and oiled wood, the knock of the pulleys against the mast, and the fluttering pennants. With all this adoration, you'd think I might have developed into a fine sailor but it was not to be. That jack-of-all-trades personality didn't work where sailing was concerned.

Being children of wartime, it was natural that we all wanted to play at combat and wear uniforms. I liked the look of the sailor's uniform and was very disappointed that we had no sea cadets in our town to join. I decided that I would become a member of the local squadron of daring air cadets instead. After I joined that junior birdman force I was quite pleased to discover that boating was part of the activities. Each weekend I would get a bonus. I'm not sure why, but instead of getting to fly in a plane they would take us out on Lough Neagh in roaring powerboats.

As usual, I ended up in the water, fully clothed and wearing one of those dreadful, scratchy wool tunics. They managed to pull me out when they realized I was going down for the third time. It was then I decided that I'd better learn to swim if I was going to go to sea. I had a dull, sinking feeling that more dark water was in my future. A little voice in a seashell told me to get prepared.

After the war, there was a glut of army surplus materials in Ireland. It seemed that everyone I knew wore something khaki. I'm sure the expression "Yer Granny wears army

Junior birdman, wishing I was a sea cadet

boots" came from our town because used military goods appeared everywhere. My next marine adventure came courtesy of that front when our Da got a job with a Mr. Danker, who operated an army surplus warehouse. I heard my father telling my mother that his boss was a "miserable oul twister" who wore a sly look on his face all the time and spoke in an excitable German-sounding accent. Behind his back everyone laughed at him for he looked a lot like a caricature of Adolf Hitler. He combed a long wisp of hair across his bald head that would fly in the wind like a bird's wing and made him look even madder than he was.

Mr. Danker was very bossy to my happy-go-lucky little Da. Since jobs were not easy to come by my father worked endless unpaid overtime hours for this merchant of war goods. I was allowed to visit the old storage sheds when the boss was away. What a treasure trove for a boy with a warrior's imagination! I could be Admiral Mountbatten, General Montgomery, or Rommel the Desert Fox.

One day when my Da was busy sorting through new shipments, I explored the contents of one of the outer sheds and, to my delight, I discovered an inflatable two-man life raft. When I pulled it out of its wooden box, I found that the camouflaged craft carried a pump, and after what seemed like hours of hard pumping, she was tight. Fumbling with excitement, I started rummaging through some survival pockets and found a knife, a whistle, brown tins full of God knows what, a tentlike cover that could be fitted over the top, as well as a fine pair of folding paddles. Ready for war, I sat aboard under the cover with the rain hammering the tin roof of the shed, and the smell of oily canvas in my ever-sniffy nose. That longing to be afloat was tugging at me again. Messing about in boats . . . messing about . . . messing . . . messing, whispered the wind in the willows.

Of course, I would never venture into any mission without Harry, my small comrade in arms. With his shock of red hair and streak of wildness, Harry was always willing to be the first to sign up for my next adventure. On the spot our commando raid was planned. Old Ruben Danker was off to England for a week leaving me Da in charge of the store. It was easy enough to drag the inflatable out the back gate and carry it off to the battlefront. This was a commando raid behind enemy lines.

Our planned objective was to cross the big pond in the people's park. All's fair in love and war, they say, and I felt very little guilt about borrowing the war boat. Anyway, I reasoned, we'd have it back before anyone knew it was missing! Wrong again. I still hadn't learned that my middle name was Jonah.

Luckily, there were no whales in the park pond to swallow me. However, there were other dangers ready to be negotiated.

*Harry and
me looking for trouble*

We landed on the muddy bank with fierce cries to scatter the enemy. Our adversaries were a big flock of ducks and a couple of swan generals, and we used a bag of stale bread to lure them out into the water away from the safety of their reedy bunkers. Once we had them out in the open water, they were transformed into minesweepers and small battleships, hot on our trail. What could we do but bombard them with chestnut grenades collected on the park pathways?

Mouthing frightening explosions we "sank" quite a few of those feathered destroyers and were enjoying the fray immensely until the great rout took place. Harry noticed with horror that a small green rowboat was putting out from the far shore. Now this was the real enemy: park keeper General Doom. He was the one who officially put locks on the swings after five p.m. and all day Sunday. He knew Harry the red man and I from a few previous skirmishes. We were indeed the enemy. The old park keeper's furious rowing was churning up the water, and we didn't need to see the look on his face to know that wild hatred was boiling inside him, hatred pent up and stored for small boys who dared to enter his park domain. Revenge was in his demeanor like something tangible. We could imagine his mutterings: "Didn't all my signs read clearly? NO BOATING, SWIMMING OR FISHING! Couldn't the little worms read?!" "Come back here!" he screamed at the top of his lungs. "Don't move!" he added in frustration.

His fat, round, freckled face reminded me of a pig's and his lips pouted out above a chinless neck. He had lost an eye in some battle in a bar and one of the lenses of his round wire glasses was painted black to hide the fact. He was typical of those old ex-servicemen who got government jobs after the war as parking attendants or wardens of public places and government buildings. To these old sergeants and corporals the war was still on and their training could not tolerate insubordination from the ill-trained public sector. He wore some sort of a military jacket and a Royal Navy sea captain's hat over his bald pate and the hat rested on his cauliflower ears. I'm sure he thought his uniform made him look official, with the cap an expression of pride from his experience on the cross-channel ferry service. I always thought he looked like a bus conductor, and when I think of him now the face of Benny Hill comes to mind.

We had a mutual hatred for each other and his chief goal was to prevent us "slippery little bastards from the town" from having any fun in his park. Our manifesto it seems was to evade capture while we climbed trees, picked flowers, kicked soccer balls on his well-cut lawns and threw skipping stones over the small lake in his park kingdom.

Now he had us on the run! We could hear him yell, "You little bastards, you dare to bring an army boat onto my water!" He was roaring out some other strange war chants as he drew closer to our gunboat. In near terror I almost leaped into the pond and our paddling became more frantic. We were out of rhythm, splashing like mad to evade our formidable enemy. A whole string of waterfowl also joined the chase, looking for more spoils from our "crumby" war games.

We tried to make it to the far shore where a wall and steps up from the dam led out onto the back streets of the town. Unfortunately, it was here that a rather dangerous outfall of the dam was controlled. We called the place the "Devil's Cup" and it resembled a big stone bowl. The water from the dam poured out here in a muddy green cascade, falling about twenty feet before it hurtled into the local river. Now it was about to hurtle two small warriors, caught in the current, into that same river. We had once seen a dead dog swirling around down there, and I could imagine our frail little bodies suffering the same fate.

The raft sped toward that awful opening and bounced into the iron grillwork placed there to stop debris from falling through. This time we were the debris. The inflatable pronged into a spike and made a sound like the devil hissing through his teeth. The park warden, now almost on top of us, was also hissing and wheezing like a steam engine. We grabbed the grill and hung on for our lives.

Our gallant vessel, now a pile of canvas rags, was dragged down beneath the grill and poured into the dark tunnel that led to the sea. At first our hunter just sat gulping for air in the green rowboat, holding himself by an iron ring in the stone wall. Then a wild tirade of abuse and curses spewed from his mouth that would have made the devil himself wince. When he had calmed down a bit and got a burst or two more salvos out of his system, he noticed that we were now reduced to terrified children crying for help.

The thought of being sucked under that grill and tumbled down into hell had turned the bravest of commandos into very small boys. Colonel Doom hauled us into his boat, and we were forced to listen with nodding heads and devout attention to his mad sermon all the way back to his keeper's cabin. Then the whole sordid marine adventure was related to my poor wee Da. That ever kind and patient man performed a few radical ravings of his own when he found out about the theft and the loss of the inflatable. All hell broke loose and I was told never to visit the surplus warehouse again. My father lost his job shortly after that, although I don't believe it had anything to do with the sunken inflatable. I'm sure that my most honest of fathers would never have told the boss that his son was a buccaneer. The place burned down less than a year later and, with a touch of poetic justice, my father had joined the local volunteer fire brigade and helped control the war surplus inferno.

FOURTH VERSE

The testing of wobbly sea legs

On my eleventh birthday we were preparing to move once more. This time there would be no argument from me. We had to take up residence in my favorite seaside town of Portrush, where we had spent summer holidays, in a caravan owned by my Uncle Joe. I loved the idea of living at the sea, but my parents were upset by the planned move. This time it might be more than a year before Granda had another house in town for us to renovate.

There is no place on earth to me quite like that Celtic coast on a fine day. The water sparkles for miles and white limestone headlands reflect the sunlight. One of the finest and most dramatic ruins in all of the British Isles covers the top of a high cliff. With its colorful history, Dunluce Castle was an exceptional playground for any boy who ever lived. We locals believed that just below the castle in the cold dark waters, a Spanish galleon lay wrecked and full of treasure. We would point out the spot to tourists who smiled at our quaint way of talking and our fairytales. Later, I was very satisfied to learn that some Dutch divers listened to the "oul wives' tales" and sent down a dive team on the spot that was known to the coastal folk. Sure enough they found the wreck. The treasure is

*Our
mystery
sailor's
grave*

stored in the Ulster Museum in Belfast and I never grow tired
of visiting that exciting display.

Near that rented caravan on the cliffs was a sailor's grave
that nestled in a little sheltered nook cut into the coarse grass
and sandy hillside. Beneath the sea-grass sod was buried the
body of a sailor. My father told us that he was washed up
during the war and was buried on the spot where they found
his body. That unknown mariner haunted our seaside holidays
for my Uncle Joe said there hadn't been a lot of him left after
the fish had finished with him. The thought of his eyeless
corpse kept me from eating anything fishy until I was well into
my twenties!

We were all caretakers of that little grave. Every summer a
new crop of children would place white limestone pebbles
around the border, and years ago someone had laid out the
design of an anchor. The Irish have a grand respect for the

dead, and I was pleased to discover on a recent visit that the sailor's grave was still there, almost unchanged in forty years.

By the summer of my twelfth birthday we were living full time in the railway carriage near that grave and I became the man of the family for a while. My mother in frustration had sent our unemployed father off to England to work on the "buildings." While my mother took work in the guest houses in town, I had to cook the meals and haul coal, water, and food across the seaside fields and down the hillsides from the nearest shop a mile and a half away.

There was not much time for sailing fun, but I did learn to row that year in the damaged rowboat my Uncle Joe had discarded after the wedding mishap. He had simply pushed the heavy old boat under the rental caravan, and my mother had plans to use it as a flower planter. When I finally maneuvered it out from under a couple of years of junk, I thought it was a fine, sleek, seaworthy-looking boat indeed.

Old Dan Hannoway, the drunken fisherman who had helped me rescue the rowboat out of the harbor, was still there. He kept his boat moored in Portrush and, as he had promised, he showed me how to "cork" a wooden boat. I watched him working one day on his own boat outside the harbor bar with six bottles of Guinness lined up along the upturned hull of his dory. The kind of man who believes in mixing work with great pleasure.

Dan first cut out a broken piece of plank and replaced it with a new one. After a good deal of shaping with a small hand plane, he made it watertight with a can of hot pitch, boiled on the open fire in the pub. Next he took a soft cotton rope and deftly rolled it out and stuffed it into the cracks with a hammer and cold chisel. "This is dead easy," I thought. Dan loaded me up with some of the pitch and cotton twist in exchange for carrying two more dark pints from the bar to the boat. I was on my way to starting my apprenticeship in caulking a wooden boat. Off I went home to work on my own boat. Without the benefit of the Guinness the task was a mighty struggle of frustration. The rope would not go in the cracks, the hot pitch was splashing everywhere, and by the time the job was even half done I looked like I had been tarred and feathered.

I crawled under the boat to check for daylight shining through the hull. I was satisfied to see only a few little peeps of light showing and I thought that the job wasn't bad for a beginner. My mother was hanging laundry in the fresh sea breeze, and as she passed my job site I popped out from under the boat. She let out a wild squeal of shock when she caught sight of the tarry apparition emerging from under the boat. Her laundry basket dropped upside down on a patch of tar I had left behind. When she gained her composure, I received a fair crack over the ear and was sent to boil water for the Saturday night, whether-we-needed-it-or-not ceremony in the big tin tub bath.

When all was calm and clean once more, I made two oars out of wooden poles fitted with tin blades. The big tidal pools were alive with creatures of the deep and, in my young mind, I would soon be entering

An early love—I found her adrift at sea

the gateway that led to the adventures of Ulysses. If those little pools were swarming with such incredible swimming things, just imagine what lay out there in the deep! Were there really fish that could fly? Did whales and dolphins really talk to each other? I had read that in Australia, where some of my uncles lived, a Great Barrier Reef sheltered sea snakes that were deadly poison, rockfish that looked like chunks of rock and had venom as deadly as that of a cobra, and sharks as long as houses. Down there the waves curled in on the beaches like liquid mountains.

Along my Irish shoreline we had very little to fear from the fish kingdom. It was the cold stormy waters that needed respect. On my first few ventures out in the resurrected rowboat I kept close to the shore or the harbor wall, and full of the pleasure of lapping wave and dipping tin blades, I paddled and sailed away that twelfth summer. Then on the last week of the holidays, with the brick walls of the old school already closing over my freedom, I made my daring plan in defiance of the long boring months of militant education.

I remember having a bad dream about that sailor's grave on the night before I decided to sail off on my big adventure. I saw the ocean open in a kind of whirlpool and some horrible fishy thing slither out of the hole to chase me. Perhaps I had tried eating some of those raw limpets so favored by one of my uncles.

I rigged a small mast onto the freshly caulked boat, and with a torn piece of canvas I found at the harbor I set a sort of sail that would catch the wind like the sail of a Chinese junk. The voyage that had been charted in my mind all of August was launched and, feeling like a Norse invader, I pushed off on a wild adventure to the big sea cave in the cliffs near the ruins of Dunluce Castle.

I had seen old photos of Victorian tourists being rowed into the awesome mouth of the cave. It was called Portcoon, and Dan had told me all about the place and how he used to make a bit of money rowing people into the cave at low tide. I really had no idea how far it was from the Portrush harbor, but I felt confident when he said, "Oh, ye'd have no bother to row there and back." So with this easy assurance, I set out on my voyage of discovery on one of those deceivingly calm and beautiful north Irish mornings, deciding it was now or never. It would be a solo attempt since all my mates had headed back to their winter quarters. In a way I was glad because I wanted to test my own wobbly sea legs. The leaks were almost conquered, I had a picnic basket aboard, and I was filled with a delicious quiver of excitement.

"No problem," I thought. "Just an easy row out of the harbor, keeping close to shore, past the white rocks, and round the cliffs to the cave." I started to whistle a jaunty jig, and the wind seemed to be joining in for it too started to whistle, ever so slightly at first, just as I pulled out of the harbor mouth.

The tide was flowing out to sea taking me along. I never counted on this development. Instead of hugging the sea wall and the cliff, the unwieldy dingy was now wallowing like an old bathtub; no longer sleek and beautiful, she was floundering in the gray-green swells. With a snap, my makeshift mast and rotten canvas broke off and draped itself all over me. I shook it loose and the rope caught around my throat, almost throttling me as it dragged in the water, still tied to the boat.

The god of the perfect blue calm was now gathering arms full of gloomy clouds from the Highlands of Scotland. The weather is notorious in that corner of the sea. It comes out like a whispering ghost and before an hour has rolled by, there can be screaming banshees on your tail. That gathering wind was having no trouble at all drowning my whistling jig and me along with the tune.

That same hardy Viking who'd set out to conquer the world a short time earlier had been transformed into a small, red-haired boy with ruddy nose and greenish face. The situation was more deadly since life jackets were not plentiful in those days, and despite my best intentions I still had not learned to swim. The dream about the sailor's grave crept in to augment my fears, and one of my mother's stories about the islanders off the west coast of Ireland came creeping back to me as well. They wore unique family patterns knitted into heavy wool sweaters. Why? So their families could identify the bodies of those unfortunates who drowned at sea. I realized with horror that I was wearing the same kind of Aran sweater!

The tub tumbled about and started to take in water, both through the cracks between the planks and from the great slaps of waves hitting her broadside. I tried to scoop water out with a tin can as I had given up trying to row and was now hanging on for the life of me. The waves seemed to be battering from all directions. It felt as if I was on one of those big cup-and-saucer fairground rides, the ones that spin you around and you can never guess which way they will turn. Round and round and up and down! This ride was not fun; this ride could be my last big ride.

I thought about the little girl drowning in my old river, and I wondered if my mother and father would walk around the harbor handing out pamphlets at the spot where I had last been seen alive. Knowing my mother and her quick temper, she would probably walk around with sandwich boards announcing to all the visiting children, "Do not be damn stupid like my son. Stay out of boats unless you know how to handle them" or some such religious warning.

I remembered an old man who had been gored by a bull telling my father about his near-death experience and how he had seen his whole life flash before him. I started flashing my whole life before me, but there was not a real glut of it, so all I could think of to do at that present moment was shriek out a high-pitched cry for help to anyone, human or angel, who would listen. Luckily at twelve years of age, the concept of dying by drowning is not as vivid as when you are forty. I know this for a fact; I'll tell you that story later.

This was not the first time in my young existence that some protecting angel had come and touched my life, and it would certainly not be the last. I am not sure what the presence is that takes the time to check in on me in times of dire need, but I am convinced that I have been graced with a visit on some very important moments. I call him or her St. Anthony, and I would like to apologize here and now if I have got the wrong name and say a thousand thanks to that special angel of whatever name for giving me time to tell the tale.

Just off the shore, outside the harbor, a cluster of rocks and sand forms a small island aptly named Skerry Rock. That guardian spirit was with me this day. The boat was heading straight for the last piece of dry land before the big sea took over, and without thinking I threw myself out of the sinking bathtub dory toward the nearest slippery rock. Like a half-drowned cat thrown in a pond, I clawed and slithered over slimy seaweed scattering crabs and cormorants in my frantic determination to touch dry land. The benevolent hand of a big roller helped me onto the beach and, with a triumphant shudder, the old tub spun around a couple of times then headed out toward Scotland or America or most likely Davy Jones's locker.

After the initial cold shock of the dunking, I scrambled up to the top of the sand dune. To my great relief a fisherman was working his nets close in on the sheltered side of the rocks. He got quite a fright when a small, water-logged boy appeared out of the sea yelling like all the sea serpents of the deep were in pursuit. He got me into his boat and offered me a pair of his very large overalls and a hot cup of tea. It wasn't long before I started feeling my old self again.

I helped him with his net for a while, and we landed two beautiful, silvery salmon. By the time I strolled off his ship I had assumed the role of a hardy fisherman just in with my harvest. The town would celebrate tonight as the finest catch of the year reached the dock. The two of us were singing "Fiddlers' Green," a song about the place where sailors go if they die ashore.

Wrap me up in me oilskins and jacket
No more on the docks I'll be seen
Just tell me oul ship mates I'm taking a trip mates
And I'll see you some day in Fiddlers' Green

That of course was not the last time I was beached; it was only a rehearsal for bigger beachings to come. If that small boat had not been somehow directed onto Skerry Rock I might have gone to my own sailor's grave on some lonely landfall of the world. Dan Hannoway used to sing about a sailor's grave.

In Davy Jones's locker beneath the heaving wave,
There are bones and skulls aplenty, for it is the sailor's grave.

I am intrigued with the language of sailors. Who was Davy Jones anyway? Old Dan told me it was the final grave of drowned sailors and sunken ships. He said originally it was a Negro slave term, Duffy Jonah's locker. Duffy meant ghost and Jonah of course the luckless old salt from the Bible. I think I would prefer to end up in that "Fiddlers' Green" where,

I don't want a harp nor a halo—not me,
Just give me a ship and a good rolling sea.
And I'll play me old squeezebox as we sail along,
With the wind in the rigging to sing me a song.

I'd like to think I could end my days in that salty old place and not in some religious heaven where white-faced souls walk around with wings playing hymns on harps. I want to be with the old boys of the sea, where an old squeezebox, played by me Da, will be the only holy music I need. Where there will be a motley crew made up of every seafarer I ever knew, spending their days telling yarns and tall tales. Very rarely would we venture out into those purgatory oceans. Somehow we'd manage to keep our hulls from hell's fires as well as from the Elysian seas of heaven.

FIFTH VERSE

The saga of the emigrant calypso sailors

W hen I was seventeen, our family took the emigrant route from Ireland to Canada, a journey that started with an all-day train ride to Cork City. Then it was a midnight tender from the Cove of Cork to a floating hotel lying three miles out in the bay. Every image of that vivid time is firmly implanted in my mind. There is an old photograph of my mother, brother, and sister

Ma, my sister Sandra, and George off to America

captured forever in that moment in time, looking a bit lost aboard the big ship bound for New York City. It was a time that we would eventually recognize as one of the most exciting and confusing of our lives. It was the mid-fifties and we were probably the last of the poor immigrants leaving by ship on the ten-pound-sterling, assisted-passage immigration schemes. Like the multitudes before us, we were searching for a dream in the new land far and away across the broad Atlantic.

The mighty *Georgic* had served Cunard well and now it was making its final run. It was the end of the White Star liners and with them went some beautiful ships and a whole way of life. Immigrants are now flying across the Atlantic, and the big liners have been turned into scrap or "Love Boats" for the wealthy.

I had the time of my life for more than a week aboard that liner, exploring every part of the ship I could find. I would sneak up to the first-class deck in the afternoon and lie on one of the polished oak deck chairs. There I would pull the blanket up to my chin imagining that I was the sickly son of some industrialist. My disguise must have worked for I was offered tea and cake by the stewards who made the rounds to those pampered few on the upper deck every afternoon for tea.

Everyone around me was heaving while the ship was hawing. I will always remember the thrill of being on deck at night, leaning out over the rail to watch the giant wake roll away behind us. The dark Atlantic had a mysterious luminescence as the ship churned and foamed its way to the new world. The lights from the cabins shining out on that vast expanse of ocean gave me a long-remembered thrill, and years later, during a brief but lonesome night-time voyage, I would recall that Atlantic crossing and the many hopeful people on board the big Cunard liner.

We settled into our new Canadian world and I was transformed, almost overnight, into a North American teenager. It was the most impressionable time in my life. Our first rather humble home was on the outskirts of Toronto at Mimico Beach on Lake Ontario, and it made me feel as if I was close to the ocean again. I spent many afternoons just sitting on the rocks watching the regattas off the shores of Toronto.

Canada in the 1950s was Louis St. Laurent; it was the Palace Pier and CHUM Radio with Al Boliska playing all the good old rock 'n' roll music. It was Rocket Richard and Hurricane Hazel and sunny days at Sunnyside, that great amusement park with its big swimming pool. The old Sunnyside has been bulldozed over long ago, but to this day the smell of hamburger frying with onions will bring me back to those early Canadian experiences: the Exhibition on humid Toronto days and first kisses with girls in crinoline skirts, saddle shoes, and ponytails. I joined a fraternity with a Greek name at a high school that seemed like the American movies I'd seen in Ireland come to life. Later I spent early mornings at 6 a.m. trying to learn to row at rowing clubs near Sunnyside. We were young Argonauts of the dawn as we streaked across the limpid breakwater near the exhibition grounds chasing the ghost of the great Irish-Canadian oarsman, Ned Hanlan from Toronto Island.

It was within these settings that I made a good friendship with Bryan Evans—another sea-dreamer like me. We seemed to relate to each other immediately, perhaps because he too was a new immigrant from our British Islands. He was a tall, good-looking Londoner and truly a ladies' man, with piercing blue eyes, a grand ducktail hairdo, and, to complete the effect, a fine set of Elvis sideburns. We compared notes on both the art of girls and sailing, and I was pleased to discover that here was a more experienced skipper all round. His father had enrolled him in sailing lessons, and he was the only male in an all-girl sailing class. Yes, I thought, this is just the man to offer the job of first mate on my dream ship!

There was a lot of talk that first year around the school about tramp steamers. We heard that you could travel the world at very little cost by working on old freighters, so we filled out forms and had photos taken and sent it all away to New York. Then we sat back and waited hopefully for our first posting on a voyage to Morocco or maybe the Tasman Sea and New Zealand. We never did get a reply and so we stowed our Jack London fantasy in the hold and schemed about more available marine adventures.

We spent part of that summer of 1958 taking a few lessons on sailing dingies on Lake Ontario. Of course, the sea gremlins sensed I was once more afloat and decided something odd would have to happen, even during those innocent outings. Bryan and I had gone offshore just a little too far during one of these lessons and had bumped into a log. It seemed to be stuck to our rudder, so I leaned out to push it away with an oar. To my absolute horror I saw the strange, hollow face of a drowned woman.

It was like a scene from some fright movie and I flashed back to my dream of the sailor's grave. The poor creature had been in the water for some time, and I was transfixed by the sight of her strands of long dark hair floating out from that dreadful yellowed face. We had to stay there until the harbor patrol came and removed the body. It took a long time to erase that sight from my superstitious late-night dreams. I never did find out who she was or under what circumstances she had come to such a horrible end.

Those early Canadian years rushed by in an excitement of hot summers and frigid winters. We got our first family car, an old 1950 Pontiac, and traveled every weekend with picnic boxes, swimming gear, and musical instruments to parks and lakes. There, dozens of other new Irish families were also blending into the Canadian lifestyle, and jigs and reels would rattle the Ontario countryside for miles around.

But another kind of music was also taking hold. It was "Bee Bop A Lu La," blue jeans and hot rod cars, *Rebel Without a Cause*, rock 'n' roll, soda shops, and drive-in theaters. American teenage movies were very popular when I was growing up in Ballymena; now I felt as if I was playing a part in one. For a while I imagined that I looked like James Dean when I probably looked more like Woody Allen.

Our poor Irish upbringing meant there was no expectation from our parents to go into university after high school. It was time to get some work to help support the family in the new country. I am sad to say that I truly wanted to leave school anyway and be free. "Work for the night is coming," as my mother sang in her Ulster work ethic hymn. So, to her satisfaction, I started the search through industrial Toronto for my future career in a factory office.

My mate Bryan and I had been developing a grand scheme over the year to find a sailboat and go off on a voyage to the West Indies. In fact it was more than a scheme; it had become my passion. Of course, this did not fit into the family plan for me. I knew that once I got a job it would be good-bye to our sailing plans. Every young man I knew in the late fifties in Ontario was caught up in the desperate climb to the top of the corporate ladder.

My mother wanted to see her son wearing a nice "soft hat," carrying a briefcase, and heading off every morning on the streetcar bound for a good office job on Bay Street. She had given up hope long ago of my choosing a career as a clergyman, or even an evangelist preacher. Her dreams were somewhat fulfilled when I landed a job as a consignment clerk at the Goodyear rubber company. "Now you'll be rolling along," laughed my Da as I gloomily and dutifully punched a time clock and spent each day of my late teens sorting mail and learning the rubber tire trade for fifty dollars a week.

There I sat every day at the same desk, wearing my pinstriped shirt with the fake gold pin holding down the ends of the collar and a designer tie (Honest Ed's, two for five dollars) whose thin end always hung down longer than the wide one. The thick neck of George Wall sitting at the desk in front of me was not an inspirational sight and I was desperate for escape.

Poor old George had been a consignment clerk with the company for twenty years. He had two dress shirts and half the week he would wear the tired white one and the other half, a faded blue. His shirt collars didn't sport a jaunty pin like mine, they flew out with two frayed little wings at the end. George had one tie and it had several accumulated coffee stains from ten years of dripping. The back of the collars on both shirts were worn thin, his hair suffered the same fate, and what was left of it was greasy at the back. Skin eruptions always seemed poised, ready to burst on the edge of the collars.

I hated the back of George's neck. It cried out boredom to me. It mourned for lost youth and sexual pleasures. It whispered to me that he had never felt a soft caress or tasted a wind that smelled of coconuts and limes coming in off an emerald sea. I hated George Wall, but not for his neck or collars, or boring life. It was because he told me that if I would hang in there with the company for as long as he had, I could count on a great pension and three times the salary I was making now—for life.

Unbeknown to my long-suffering mother, the only thing in that impressive briefcase she had bought me for Christmas was my lunch and a book on the fundamentals of seamanship.

On the inside lid was a sticker that read "I'd rather be sailing."
"You stick to that job, my boy," said my poor wee Ma beaming,
"and you will become the manager of that department."
"Then," she would add with great satisfaction, "you could work
yourself all the way to the top office if you really want to."

Bryan got a similar job in a nearby factory that sold car
parts, and we both started talking in earnest about getting a
boat and setting off on our great adventure. As I traveled the
streetcar route along Queen Street every morning, I scanned
the newspaper for "Boats for Sale." The West Indies were
calling us to their verdant shores away from that flat tire office
and the silent people who kept the Canadian driver rolling on
steel-ribbed whitewalls.

I lived with the dream day and night of white sails billowing
through warm Caribbean waters and the sound of a steel drum
playing the background music. My walls were covered with

With this hat, my tropical dreams had to come true

pictures of tropical splendor, collected from the local travel office. Before sleep and for a good part of my waking day, the vision played in my thoughts. I'd be standing in the bow of a white sailing ship that had just skimmed through an opening in the coral reef. Careening down the creamy rollers in a surfing glide, the boat would traverse a turquoise lagoon to a sun-bleached village of palm trees where beautiful brown-skinned maidens waved to us from the shore.

Fortunately, the dream was always locked in that still-life frame. There was no vision of how we would manage to get to that point, what we would do to survive, or how we might get back again. Always the one scene replayed over and over. That's always been my answer, I suppose, to any troubles that have tried swamping my enthusiasm for life. I strive to capture the moment of bliss, keeping only that clear picture in my mind and ignoring all the sea monsters waiting to swallow me in the stagnant waters of practical consequence.

Fired up with our dream, we started saving money every way we could. The fifty a week from Goodyear didn't last long after I paid my mother a small pittance for room and board, and bought records and clothes to keep up with my new office career. I was also paying off my first decent guitar at twenty-five dollars a month. Songs of the West Indies were very popular that summer, so we formed a calypso trio, with our third would-be crewman a tall, skinny Welshman called Keith from the Goodyear mailroom to shake the maracas.

The factory radio was pulsing out those tropical rhythms with songs like "All Day All Night, Marianne" and silly lyrics like "day-o" and "hill and gully rider." We were the eager crew of the *Tropical Express* looking for a passage out of the rubber jungle to paradise and we jumped on the bandwagon. Down we went to the pawnshops on Jarvis Street and bought a long wooden conga drum and some maracas. I had my new guitar, and soon we were "jumping in de line and shaking our body in time." A new calypso band was born with a sailing agenda.

The practicing started in earnest, and we used to rehearse in a small Morris Minor parked in the dark on a side street beside Lake Ontario. A policeman checked us out one night when he saw a rocking car with steamy windows and inside three frantic musicians singing "Man smart, woman smarta" in a tangled mess of arms and legs, conga and bongo drums, flying maracas, and flailing guitar. After listening for a minute or two, he said, "Don't give up yer day jobs, boys," quietly switched off his light, and went away shaking his head in wonder at all the weird people he met on his beat.

We did, however, make some money with our calypso rhythms. We learned every song Harry Belafonte ever recorded and thought we sounded pretty damn good. If Mr. Belafonte had caught our act, I'm sure he would not have felt threatened by the Tropical Express: a very white, red-headed Irish teenager, a conga-beating Londoner, and a long, skinny Welshman shaking a pair of maracas—all of us yelling out "day-o day-o."

Nevertheless we won a few talent shows and got a job singing in a small hotel lounge in the suburbs of Toronto. I learned a lot of skills during my calypso career that would become the education for my future life on stage as an entertainer and leader of the Irish Rovers for thirty years or more.

When I reflect on my whole life's adventure so far, my love of boats was the catalyst for my success in entertaining. As the savings grew a little healthier, we started the exciting task of searching for our dream boat. We scoured the papers and the local boatyards around Lake Ontario, looking for the ship that would hopefully carry us away, over the sea beyond the rubber tire horizon. Away from the cold winds and bare trees to palms and papaya and yellow birds. The songs and the rhythm were the drug that drove us on.

Then we found our potential passport to paradise. The newspaper ad described just what we were looking for:

"READY FOR SAIL" The *Malahini*, thirty-two-foot sloop, fully rigged, newly rebuilt engine, sound and beautiful. Only $3,500 for freedom on the water.

The rather out-of-focus newsprint photo showed what looked like a fine sturdy sloop under sail. Thirty-five-hundred dollars was a lot less than we had saved, and it was a gigantic sum in the late fifties. "Don't worry, boys," the owner urged us on the phone. "We can make a deal if you come down right away." He convinced us that because he needed to move the boat that weekend he would give us a "swe-eet" deal.

I lay sleepless the night before we were to buy her and replayed my arrival into the tropical sunshine. The Ontario winds of October were warning of a long winter ahead, and my kit bag and guitar were packed. The *Malahini* meant newcomer in Hawaiian. Well-named, I thought, because the new owners were still strangers to a real boat and any kind of offshore cruising.

She was lying in Port Maitland on Lake Erie and the plan was carefully worked out; we were to meet the owner there on Sunday morning, deliver the money, get the papers, and sail down the lake to the mouth of the Welland Canal, through the canal, into Lake Ontario, then across to Port Credit on the other side.

Once in Port Credit we planned to stock her with supplies and outfit her for our voyage, which as far as I could understand would take us along the mighty St. Lawrence River through Quebec and out into the open sea. We would follow the coast south, past New York and Virginia. Then when we got down to Florida, we speculated that we could probably spend a couple of weeks in some place like Fort Lauderdale making money playing white calypso music.

Then, finally, the *Malahini* would carry us to the Spanish Main. At last I'd be standing sunburned and heroic at the prow as we glided down the long waves into a tropical lagoon. Perhaps the local papers would be out on the dock to take our photographs as we got an impromptu limbo dance happening on the dockside.

When the long-awaited Sunday morning dawned overcast and cool, I experienced the first of my misgivings. My regular job at the tire company was promising a raise to sixty-five dollars a week. How could I shatter my mother's delusions of grandeur, tell her I was quitting, and sail off to the tropics on a wooden sailing boat I had paid for in part by selling the car she had arranged for me with borrowed money from the dreaded buy-now-pay-forever finance companies? The hard-working woman would have had a breakdown of some sort right there on the spot.

Regardless of all the consequences that might occur, we set off early with bags full of provisions we thought we might need to clear the Welland Canal. On the drive down to Port Maitland we sang sea chanteys and talked nautical talk in Long John Silver Bristol accents. "Avast and belay there, matey, and shiver me timbers." We were so caught up in the excitement and youthful zest of our big adventure that we did not see the police car until he pulled alongside us and blasted his horn. We stopped singing and beating the conga drum. Keith pulled his long legs in the window, and I hid the small bottle of rum that every true sailor carries for emergencies at sea. Luckily it was not open, and when he found out we were going to buy a sailboat, he tried to sell us his homemade plywood dingy. We got off without a speeding ticket and started the madness once more as soon as he was out of sight.

We were greeted at the dock by a rather shifty-looking sort of fellow. He offered us a wet-fish handshake as he led us along a shaky old dock and showed us the *Malahini* for the first time. Her appearance fitted the whole shabby-looking dock area. A decrepit dingy was tied to the stern half submerged and filled with empty tin cans and debris.

The *Malahini* herself left us feeling a bit deflated. "I was going to give her a new paint job before you arrived," he said with a smile, "but so many people have been here looking at 'er that I haven't had time and I'm caring for my sick auntie in Hamilton. But don't worry. We can knock a hundred or so off the price and you can do your own color." He reminded me of a stage undertaker, and he even spoke like Boris Karloff on a bad day. I watched him rub his hands together as if to say, "Come on boys, let's deal and I'll get on my way back to my auntie's death—I mean bedside."

I stood and stared at our dream ship for a while with my two shipmates. Thirty-two feet seemed a lot bigger when we had stepped it out on the lawn a few weeks earlier. Now it looked more like eighteen. The *Malahini* had a rundown appearance and the engine resembled a pile of rusted scrap.

Sensing our disappointment, the owner went into his best auto salesman routine. He cranked up the engine and it fired with a mighty puff of blue smoke, but settled down to a noisy rattle. He hoisted up a jib sail and the main and showed us a bag of dirty-looking canvas. He looked around mysteriously and half whispered as if to share a secret. "Did you boys know that the word canvas comes from a Greek word, 'kannabis,' because the first sails were made from the good old-fashioned hemp plant." He appeared to be quite proud of himself after passing that valuable piece of trivia on to us and he snorted in satisfaction at his knowledge. Too bad he hadn't instructed us more on the workings of the engine.

"Look lads," he continued in a purring voice, eyeing the envelope of money and probably saying a fervent prayer. "I would like you to have my old *Malahini*. She's seen a lot of good times with me. We've been twice to the Caribbean together, we've entertained some beautiful women aboard, and you three look like you are the very crew that can carry on our good-time tradition!" He lit up another cigarillo, which smelled like the dirty kannabis sails, adjusted his Greek sailor cap, and combed his long mustache with a tiny metal comb. Then he homed in for the kill.

The deal was struck in an hour when he took five hundred dollars off the price and handed us the papers over a cup of weak tea down in the messy cabin. I looked at our grubby pile of tens and twenties. It seemed like a huge load of hard-earned money. He counted it quickly and scooped it up out of our sight. Then he offered another clammy handshake as he climbed back to the dock. "Of course you all know how to sail." He smiled once more and I wondered if there was a note of sarcasm in his statement. "Ha, ha," we laughed, "do we know how to sail!" "Do we?" I thought, with silent gloom. He drove off with our cash after giving us a crash course on the operation of the sails and one more bit of mechanics on the inboard engine. His parting shot was to remind us to buy insurance.

The three of us puttered around the *Malahini* for a while, trying to get used to the idea that all our plans had come to pass. With a flourish we agreed that it was time to put to sea. I believe we all had a rush of insecurity as we realized we were completely unprepared to make the trip. But the cockiness of youth kicked in and half an hour later, after priming and cursing and begging the engine, it sputtered into a life of its own. Then my next-door neighbor, the fellow who had driven us to the boat and delivered us to our fates, dumped our duffel bags on the dock. "Gotta get on the road, guys. Good sailin', eh!" He gave us a cheery wave, jumped into his old car, and headed back to sanity and the city. As I watched him disappear down the marina road toward the highway and home, a twinge of panic tugged at my heart. "Run after him," cried an anxious and somewhat nervous voice in my head, "back to your cozy house and fifty-bucks-a-week job. Jesus, what will your mother say?" Bryan's voice chased my phantom conscience. "Come on mateys, why are we standing around? Let's hoist anchor and head her out."

The first half hour developed into a turmoil that would set the mood for the next week. We even had a struggle navigating the *Malahini* away from the dock. The motor sounded healthy enough while the owner had fiddled with the bloody thing; after he departed it developed a mind of its own. As we chugged away, past a few big cabin cruisers, the racket was dreadful, and the acrid smoke that spewed out of the exhaust swirled around us like a smoke screen as the engine belched and vibrated on one cylinder.

We received a few disgruntled stares as we disturbed the Sunday morning peace with our frightful propulsion. Sometimes the engine quit and we drifted around, pushing away from other boats. Then bang and churn with a curse and a prayer and we were off once more. It was all good practice for what lay ahead in the Welland Canal.

For I'm sorry to say we did make it out of the marina. Now a bigger challenge lay ahead—to sail the damn boat along the lake to the Welland Canal and somehow maneuver it through the locks and into Lake Ontario. We hoisted the jib, a breeze puffed us into action, and I felt a surge of excitement. We manhandled and cursed a lot with the mainsail till finally it found its traction and up it spread!

For a glorious hour we were flying, and I found my moment of fulfillment. Bryan was at the tiller and Keith checked maps and charts of the canal and lake. And I moved into my dream pose, standing in the prow scanning the horizon for the tropic isles or at least the Welland Canal. The big sail billowed out as the wind whistled up and we were humming along. Blissfully I gazed skyward enthralled with the workings of the sail, the blue sky, the gull cry, and the wash of waves as we dipped along. "Way-hey and up! she rises ear-lie in the morning." And we all sang together with the power and conviction of a windjammer crew on a chantey chorus.

An hour into the voyage and the peaceful daydream vanished when I noticed some marker buoys off our starboard bow. We had been following the shoreline, staying off about a quarter mile. "Bryan," I called out casually, "see those marker buoys? I think we should be on the far side of them." Before he had time to answer we had scraped bottom. With a s-crape and long scrunch, we hit the rocky shallows. The keel had driven up on flat sandstone and the *Malahini* was firmly stuck in five feet of water.

The swells lifted us off and then crashed us back down on the rocks again. Lift-bang-up-down. It felt as if the bottom were being torn out of our souls. We were being pounded flat, with no insurance to soften the blows. We tried everything to shift her off and back into deeper water with no success. We jumped into the water, up to our chests in the chill, and tried to pull her over on her side with ropes tied to the mast. The motor gave up once more and the swells kept rolling under us. Pound! Pound! Each one rattled our nerves.

A small dory came puttering along carrying two old men out fishing. Slowly they drew closer for a look at these big city yachtsmen, stuck on the rocks. "What's you boys up to?" they laughed. "Trying to scuttle yer boat?" A burst of merriment came from the two comedians. Ordinarily I would have fired back some of my street poetry and Irish repartee, but today these old "gentlemen" were our lifeboat. I called out to them.

"Can you give us a pull off these rocks?"

"Twenty bucks," said one of them. The deal was struck, a twenty-dollar note changed hands, and after a half hour of ropes and roaring engines, curses and cries of exertion, somehow the *Malahini* staggered back off the rocks into deeper water. One of our saviors waved the twenty dollars and yelled, "Come again anytime, and remember to ignore the marker buoys." My toe was twitching to kick them up the arse.

We were on track once more with the sun sinking in the smoldering sky. Dusk was floating down when we spotted the portals of the Welland Canal looming ahead. A lineup of large freighters was waiting to enter the canal system, and, being

Confusion reigns on the Malahini

first-time canal users, we didn't have a clue what to do, so we just nipped into the flow with the giant vessels towering over us. A titanic horn blast from the nearest freighter almost blew me overboard, and the *Malahini's* struggle to conquer the Welland Canal commenced.

You cannot sail through a canal, a motor is a necessity, so our problems started before we ever reached the first lock. Splutter and snort and die was the rule of the infernal machine and it became our enemy, jerking away and cutting out under our feet. We limped along in mortal dread of being rammed by the steel giants who towered behind us full of impatient cargo with no time to entertain some dryland sailors.

A friendly American yacht sped to our rescue and threw us a towline, and in the eerie darkness of that first day, those ever dependable Yankees moored us in an industrial area and waved us bon voyage. I stayed with the *Malahini* while my other two shipmates made their way ashore. I sat there glum and shivering, with a vague hatred already growing in me for this wooden relic.

As the evening progressed I developed a feverish feeling, no doubt the result of my waterlogged clothing. All around me the lights in the industrial dockyard spread gloomy shadows across the canal, and I wished I could just get to hell out of there. Alone with my tormented thoughts of the tropics and my rubber tire company employment, I decided a cup of tea aboard would do nicely, then a bit of a rest under the blanket while I waited for the crew to return. I lifted the Coleman stove from a locker and filled it from a tin of cooking fuel marked "Highly flammable—Caution!" I took the stove up on deck and set it up in the stern, unaware that it was dripping fuel all the way. When a light was added, whoosh! A nice line of flame lit up the dusky night. "Oh, Jesus!" I yelled frantically. "She'll burn down before the others return!" For a moment I mused on the idea of letting the flames gobble her, then I remembered—no insurance.

After a few jigs and jumps I started beating the deck with a wet towel. The stove was in flames and the old varnished seat was smoking. My frantic beating was not winning the battle. Lucky for me there happened to be a couple of workers on a barge nearby who jumped aboard and doused the deck with a fire extinguisher. When all was calm, they took me into their cabin on the barge and poured me an Old Navy rum and Coke, and I swallowed it down with a great splutter and cough. I wasn't much of a drinker, but now I was ready to join in their laughter. They both came from Newfoundland and we shared a couple of old songs and jokes, and when I told them we were planning to sail to the West Indies, one of them replied, "You'll be lucky, my son, to make it through the canal with that boat."

One of the fellows promised to come in the morning to try to make the engine more shipshape. I cleaned up the mess as best I could, and when my mates returned later with a hearty meal of potato chips and coffee, they commented on the smell of something burning and wondered why I was acting drunk. I didn't tell them the fireside story, but I thought to myself, "Just don't light that old stove, my boys."

Malahini Log—First day at sea (at least Canal)

Shivering with the flu I toss about in the cramped bunk, the blankets wet with dew. The weather is cold and foggy and I can't even see the stern of the boat. Wish to God I was home in my own bed. Feel like I'm in a coffin. As I stare at a moldy ceiling four inches from my face, great shadowy hulls churn past our moorage, banging us about. I'm going nuts; Keith is singing a stupid Welsh song that sounds like ya-ke-da, ya-ke-da, and Bryan is tapping time with his foot on the deck over my head, right above my face. I'm a prisoner. They are holding me hostage! I'll rot here, and never see my loved ones again. I didn't really want to run away to sea, honest! I've been shanghaied. My head is throbbing, I've developed a consumptive cough, and I need chicken soup and hot soda bread. Help!

My Newfoundland mechanic finally showed up later in the day, just as the fog was lifting and the sun was starting to warm up the deck. It looked as if it would take all the money we had in our possession to pay for the parts needed to make the motor work. We persuaded him to do a repair job just to get us through the canal, and by four in the afternoon we were waving him farewell and puffing along, approaching the first low bridge.

As the flow carried us toward the bridge, we expected it would rise up to allow our mast to clear. There was no activity from the little control booth at all. We could see the bridge keeper but he was not looking our way. We started to blow our little foghorn to alert him to raise the structure, but he must have been asleep. Just as we drew near, the engine cut out again, and once more we were drifting in the current with the mast about to smack into the bridge. When we hit, the mast bent like a bow but thankfully didn't snap. The boat turned a drunken circle just about the time the bridge keeper decided to lift the structure, and I saw to my horror that the pulley on the masthead was hooked to the bridge. We were about to be hoisted with the bridge. We had been lifted about a foot out of the water before the pulley assembly broke.

The *Malahini* drifted close enough to the sloping walls of

the canal for me to jump ashore with a rope in an attempt to make us fast. It was leap, miss, slide, and down the wall I shot, landing in the dark, messy canal water. Now I was floundering somewhere under the hull, still clutching the rope. My mates pulled me up, and for some demented reason they were roaring with wild laughter. The madness of it all had infected them. I joined in their gaiety as only the insanity of youth will allow.

Then it was another evening tied up to the canal bank, and another spell of work on the engine. We would have dearly loved to see the slippery snake who sold us the boat. We even phoned him to come and help us. "This number is no longer in service," said the voice on the other end of the line. We reckoned that by this time he was probably sipping rum from a coconut in the Virgin Islands.

There was a flurry of anticipation the next morning as we prepared to venture inside the first lock. The engine sounded fine, but we were learning quickly about this devilish, banging monster under the deck boards. It had a beast mind of its own. All went well as we were directed into the lock. We tied her up with one of our made-up knots and felt satisfied as the water level in the lock slowly started to fall.

I watched in fascination as our lines grew tight, and we dropped lower and lower with the dropping water level. No one had told us how much slack to leave tied to the dock, and before we knew it we were at the end of our rope—literally. Now the boat was about to be strung along the wall of the lock as the water poured out below. The rope was completely taut, stopping us from dropping lower with the level of the water. A lock keeper rushed over and frantically slashed at the line with a knife. Onlookers shook their heads in disbelief as we dropped with a hard splash back into the water.

This was decidedly not the stuff of my daydreams. King

Neptune was calling me aside and in fatherly tones was telling me, "Son, there are sailors and there are sailors. You had better stick to model boats and sailing books. It's okay," he whispered, "the sea is a nasty, wet, and dangerous place. Do you think if I had a motorbike and a couple of legs instead of this codfish tail I'd be down here ruling the waves? I've always wanted to retire in the desert." I think the fever was working on my imagination.

The Welland Canal quite possibly saved my life, and even though I have risked the deep now and then over the years, gone for a long time was my misguided passion for a life at sea. By the time we cleared the last lock, two more near drownings would touch me with an icy finger. During one chilling moment we froze in terror as we came within a few feet of being run over by the same rusty tanker we had encountered on our grand entrance to the canal. And we screamed wild, salty insults as we smacked the now-damaged mast against two more bridges.

I've never been a quitter, but the flu and the hazards of that peaceful canal caused this *Malahini* prisoner to escape from his gallant shipmates. At the last lock, before we headed into Lake Ontario, I made my getaway. I had heard there was a storm predicted and to my horror my shipmates were hellbent on heading out into threatening, unpredictable Lake Ontario.

I argued that we should wait until a more experienced sailor could join the crew. "Har har, Billy!" they laughed. "We be handy seamen. We'll make landfall with this here scow by the morning light!" I laughed with them and gathered up my little duffel bag. Then, with thinly disguised relief, I sadly wished them bon voyage and shivered my way up to the highway to hitchhike back to warm Sunday evening kitchens and Monday morning rubber company security.

There was an icy welcome from my family when I hove into view late in the night. My mother performed one of her best soliloquies ever. She was in top temper for the job. It mattered little that I was nineteen; she had no inhibitions about giving her growing son a good belt up the side of the ear. She went through it all—the disappointment, the rage, the "you owe me" stuff, and finally the hopeless grief, which always got to me the most. Bryan's parents had called and told her all about the boat and the West Indies plans. She was ready to commit me to any asylum that would take me in.

I hated myself in the morning for leaving my shipmates to the unknown lake crossing. I woke up at dawn from a dream of whirlpools and a ragged old ship that seemed to be the *Malahini* spinning round and round in the rushing flow. I was hanging on to a slippery steel line and was in terror that I would let go and be sucked down into the vortex. Bryan was not offering me any help, and I could feel his anger as he said, "Tough luck." Then a woman, who looked like my mother, threw me a large rubber tire—it was a whitewall— and I woke up with my heart pounding trying to put it over my head.

Outside the weather had turned miserable, and I lay there listening to the whistling wind and the rain hammering at the window. Sliding a little deeper down into the covers, I gave a shudder for that wooden sloop out there in the gray-brown waves of Lake Ontario. I had read about white squalls on the Great Lakes, and I was sure the *Malahini* had been swallowed up.

The weather eased after two days of storming, and the lake turned slick and leaden. There wasn't a breeze and my worries that the voyage had ended on the lake bottom were beginning to seem more real. Bryan's father, who had helped him put some of the financing together to buy the boat, was one of the stiff-upper-lip British types. He never seemed to be upset over teenage problems. He phoned the harbor police and after a sweeping search the *Malahini* was found becalmed, with a lifeless engine, one tin of good old Campbell's soup for sustenance, and the rigging like spaghetti from the two-day storm. My mates told me later that they thought they heard the angels sing and they were good enough to also tell me that I had been right and they should have waited.

I wasn't sure whether to be thankful to my guiding angel or not for making me leave the ship. I reasoned it out in the end that, in retrospect, we were lucky that so much trouble came down on us the first few days of the voyage. It is clear now that not one of us really wanted to continue the *Malahini* madness out into the open sea, two hundred nautical miles offshore and battling mountainous waves to get to the West Indies. I pictured us trying to fish with the last tin of Campbell's soup, with Keith singing ya-ke-da and Bryan trying to send conga drum signals to the Canary Islands over his homemade short-wave radio. With our luck, we might have made landfall in Newfoundland.

The *Malahini* was sold at a loss shortly afterward. Bryan went back to school and eventually became an Air Canada captain. His sailing for fun now takes place on small, frightening ultralights that fly powered by lawnmower engines. Bryan is the kind of man you'd like to have on your crew for any mad adventure. Keith, the tall, skinny Welshman, grew religious and plump with success in some paper products world. Our ships never crossed paths again, and now they are only small, out-of-focus figures in an old photo snapped in that first lock of the Welland Canal. I guess I am the only one of the "three boyos in a tub" who continued to pursue that dangerous quest for perfection under sail.

I have a kind of remorse inside that Bryan and Keith and I

did not make landfall in St. Thomas or Jamaica. I didn't even make it across Lake Ontario with them! That small defeat still bothers me after all this time. I have tried to make up for it ever since on other ships. Perhaps one of these days I will find Bryan and Keith again and play a few old calypso songs. Maybe even find a stout little ship and make a professional passage through the canal and across the lake. Then a galloping full sail run down the eastern seaboard to the tropical nights we used to dream about. After all these years, the youthful dreams still survive in my sailor's heart.

> *Yesterday and years ago*
> *There was a place I used to know*
> *Across the dunes a hop and skip*
> *By lime white cliffs and swirling gull*
> *Broken bones of a sailing ship.*
> *Weeds and weather crack the hull*
> *Dried out planks, sea scrubbed deck.*
> *I fixed the holes with canvas rag*
> *Sea wind croons around the wreck.*
> *Many's the day in the cabin below*
> *I charted course and hoisted flag*
> *To tropic shore and Cape Horn blow.*
> *A mile she lay from breakers' roar*
> *I sailed on fancy dry ashore.*
> *With blanket sail on broken mast*
> *Summers pass and childhood flies.*
> *The heart still holds the memories fast*
> *Till the last trip dims the sailor's eyes.*

I was sifting through the remains of my mother's life after she died and found this poem of mine in one of her hymn books. I had written it during our first year in Canada, when we were all very homesick for our old town of Ballymena. Mother sent the poem back to the editor of the newspaper there and it was printed shortly after. She had clipped the poem and kept it tucked in her hymn book at the page that contained the sailor's hymn "Let the Lower Lights Be Burning." I was glad of that. Any little spiritual help is most welcome when Neptune is out to get you.

SIXTH VERSE

The Irish Rover gets her sails and heads for Gloryland

*T*hose rubber tires were starting to roll over my heady dreams, and the calypso band played out a year of small successes in local Toronto clubs. One day at my tire order desk, while I was reading a magazine about motor sailing around the world, the boss, a big Irishman called Mr. Darmody, called me into his office. He told me that between my music and my boating he felt I had little interest in the exciting and booming rubber business.

"Son," he said in tired, fatherly tones, "the only things you have in your desk, or your head for that matter, are guitar necks and sailing books. (I had a guitar neck in my desk drawer to practice chords, and he had caught me one day playing the neck, lost in the rhythm of my imaginary guitar.) "So," he continued after one of his irritatingly thoughtful pauses, "we aren't married, are we, and it's easy to get a divorce."

"I guess you're bidding me aloha," I said smiling. "Ah, you could have been a great tire salesman, son, if you had the desire to succeed," he said, kindly enough.

Mr. Goodyear lost a great tire consignment clerk when I signed on as captain of the *Irish Rover*. I said good-bye to George Wall and to Marnie, the most desirable credit department clerk I ever had the honor to sail with. Her father owned a fine yacht on Lake Ontario, and that muscular young lady tormented my nineteenth summer in afternoon hideaways aboard the well-laid-out party boat. There was a boatload of fun and games until I put a dent in the hull of the plastic boat when I switched on the motor and accidentally hit the forward gear. Luckily, we were tied to the dock. Before Daddy found out about the damage to the hull he caught the young stowaways playing love games and threw me off his yacht. I would probably have acted the same in his shoes, and I must say he was a worthy adversary and always had a fine, healthy disregard for me and my sailing prowess. He had tolerated me on board until he discovered my dalliance with his daughter. I'm not sure if he was more upset about Marnie's virtue or the indignity committed to the hull.

I celebrated my twentieth birthday at a grand party in a new calypso club on Yonge Street in Toronto. I had become the leader of a four-piece Trinidad steel drum band (if I couldn't sail there I would bring the islands to Toronto), and I am still not sure how a white fella from Ulster could lead four Trinidadians six nights a week at a successful calypso club. However, that's what happened. We wore ruffle sleeve shirts and white pants with silly straw hats on our heads and the public who flocked to fill the place every weekend thought we were great.

My heart didn't really belong in these tropical melodies though. It was Irish music that hummed in my soul, and I was completely taken by the folk music that was very popular in the United States at that time, played by such groups as the Kingston Trio and the Limelighters. Then I discovered the Irish singing group the Clancy Brothers and Tommy Makem. They were enjoying great success in New York singing all of those old songs that I had grown up with and knew so well.

I had heard about the famous folk clubs in California and was desperate to play in one of them. So I left the calypso club like a gipsy on the run in an old beat-up Volkswagen without a heater. That horrible little car carried me across the wild, frozen wastes of the Canadian winter prairies. My plan was to make it to San Francisco, but fate was waiting for me once again as I entered Calgary in a snowstorm. My funds were almost gone when I spotted the neon sign of the Beacon Hotel as it sparked and spluttered an invitation to visit the Calypso lounge. "Well, my goodness," I thought. "A sign from my angel! The first lights I see after the long prairies call out 'calypso.'"

I parked the car and took my frozen guitar and body off to see the manager. "I'm from Ireland," I announced, "but I sing calypso and play steel drum and can I have a meal and a job? Please."

I was down to my last hundred dollars, and I believe he took pity on me and my sprouting goatee beard. He said okay to the meal (his mother was Irish), and I had barely finished bolting it down when he jumped up to the microphone and announced, "Hey folks, hope you're enjoying your steaks here at the Calypso lounge in the beautiful Beacon Hotel. Got a treat for you, a calypso singer from Ireland is our special guest tonight. Come on up here, son, and entertain the crowd." Half a dozen couples were digging into spuds and steaks. A few of them, who'd had more to drink than the others, gave a spirited round of applause and I bounded up on to the stage ready to do battle for survival. It was a bit of a struggle, but my years on Irish stages pulled me through, and before long I had them singing "All Day All Night, Marianne." I got the job and the good ship *Irish Rover* was about to be sent down the slip into the water for her maiden voyage.

From that calypso room I landed a daily TV show for children. Then my brother George and his friend Jimmy

Me, George, Joe, and Jimmy

Ferguson came to visit for a summer holiday. They would form the nucleus of the band and they never left my life for the next thirty years. With the addition of my cousin Joe, we formed the Irish Rovers. I supported them for a while with my TV show and solo singing around the tables of a pancake house. The urge to be going was tugging at me, and it was time to head to mecca—the folk clubs of California.

It was a long and jolly sail around those folky places in the mid-sixties, and then in 1969 we struck the mother lode with a hit record. The dream of every young band had come true for the Irish Rovers and I was ready for anything. It happened through a string of success in the folk clubs and our recording of a whimsical little song called "The Unicorn." Then the magic carpet was out and we tripped along it through Hollywood and TV series and sold-out concerts. Now I had my passport to the waiting world. Mind you, the mad rush of success that had settled over us often made me long for the quiet days and for peaceful uncomplicated sailing in home bays. I promised myself I would return to Ireland as soon as the career allowed.

The only safe place for boats I rent—the beach

As young men with newfound success are wont to do, I fell in love. My long-awaited travel to Australia and New Zealand came true, not under sail, as I had hoped, but by a big jet that landed us in Sydney airport. We were greeted by crowds of Irish exiles, a pipe band playing "The Minstrel Boy," and a reeling throng of Irish dancers. In typical Aussie fashion, there was even a horse with a horn on its head spreading unicorn droppings all over the airport. We had an unbelievable three songs on the Australian charts, and "The Unicorn" was number one. The sun, the celebrations, the champagne: my God, I thought I had found the promised land.

A love affair was born out of that first week of high revelry in Sydney, and she was a fine-looking, witty, and quite spirited young woman. We stayed together long enough to develop a stormy relationship that couldn't be saved. I told her of my dream of returning to Ireland to live, and she caught a taste of those dreams. We traveled back together and lived in a stone cottage at Ballycastle—a hundred-year-old, converted fisherman's cabin that faced the sea and the distant hills of Scotland.

It was a grand affair for one winter of turf fires and poetry. I was in a rush of success back in my old Irish ground and this time if you please with a few dollars in my pocket. I bought a

Rover and explored every sea corner of Ireland. While the Australian lady rode a horse around the hills of Ballycastle, I sailed across from Ballycastle many times to the ancient island of Rathlin.

I paid a fisherman on that island to help me build a good strong boat that could sail around Ireland. This was one more dream that had been stewing away on my wish list of sailing adventures. Paddy Black was the shipbuilder's name, and I felt as if I had returned to my ancient sailing roots the day he laid the keel. Paddy was an odd, mysterious fellow and came from a long line of shipbuilders and fishermen who had made that windswept island home for three or four generations. We got along well together, and I enjoyed his art of storytelling. He knew a great wealth of stories and could hold me spellbound with his Irish myths and fairy lore of Ireland's "other world."

I felt I had finally come home after the years in the heat of Los Angeles and all the flurry of recording success. I planned to make a home out of the old stone house, and I was sure we would be living there for a long time. Building the boat, I figured, would be a labor of love and I could do it at my leisure, but it was not to be. The "Troubles" started that same year, and the bombs and the army left Northern Ireland a frightening place for a fair-weather sailor to find his anchorage. I traveled away quite often to play my music, leaving the girl from sunny Australia caught in the storms of that unhappy province.

Each time I returned it seemed that we had grown further apart. I would work at the boat on Rathlin whenever I could, but it was a hopeless undertaking. The summers were usually misty, wet, and cool, and the waters were very unpredictable between Ballycastle and the island. Once you went across in the morning there was no guarantee that the boatman would bring you back the same day. It was a world far from the glitter, surrounded by towering cliffs that were blasted by the salt sea spray, the home of swirling seabirds and hardy people who seemed to need very little of modern comforts. After spending weeks alone while I was away on tour, the last thing the Australian lady wanted was more solitude.

We rode bicycles in the gales and grew more distressed with the nightly news from Belfast and Derry. The dream was fading, and my Ireland was not the place I knew and loved. I was filled with great disillusionment as we tried to understand each other's dreams and only ended up heading off on different pathways over the seas in search of tranquility. When we parted, we sold the stone house and I believe Paddy Black finished off the boat for himself.

The waters between Scotland and the North Antrim coast are very unforgiving to careless sailors. There may have been another chapter to record had I stayed and completed the *Calypso*—for that was to be the name of the new boat. (I had not yet heard of Jacques Cousteau or his million-dollar vessel of that name.) It was not meant to be and sometimes dreams are only good in the dreaming stage.

In the way of most love affairs that come to a stormy end, it was not a clean break, for memories linger on and you think that just maybe it can work one more time. I traveled back once more to Australia when another Irish Rover tour was set in motion, and for a time we tried to rekindle the flickering flame.

We spent time sailing a sloop in Melbourne called *Fantasy*. My girl from Bondi was quite a nervous sailing partner, and when I suggested an overnight sail up along the Melbourne coast she was rather hesitant. "The sky is so beautiful out there, the wind is just right," I gushed. "You'll love it." I had to assure her that it would be a wonderful night's sail, and I fully believed what I said. There were times in those distant waters when I thought the stars and the dark sea were all intertwined. The wind was a steady warm flow and I truly felt we could resurrect the old spark of love. Once we were out on the water she joined me at the tiller. I put my arm around her and was just about to whisper, "Isn't this wonderful?" when I sailed directly into a small plywood motorboat.

The noise of the collision was so dreadful out there in the calm night air that I thought I had run aground once more. I raced to the bow, wild-eyed, my heart hammering. I called out into the dark, "Is there anybody out there?" I could see no oars or outboard engine and I was relieved that it was probably just a runaway.

My relief, however, was short-lived when I realized part of the broken boat had caught in the rudder and I could not steer correctly. Then, when I started the engine, the painter (the rope tied to the front of the dingy) wrapped itself around the propeller. The wind had died to a puff or two. We were stuck out there with the sparkling lights of Melbourne half a mile astern.

I tried pushing the debris from our rudder with a long pole, but it was a hopeless task. "We have to go down there and cut the nylon rope off the propeller and drive shaft." "We, captain?" she said. "Off you go then, mate!"

I paused for a moment, thinking that perhaps I might just give it a try. Then I remembered there were sharks living in these waters, white pointy beasts with mouths that could swallow a Volkswagen. "Let's wait till morning," I said finally. "It's just a wee bit dark."

It was not the romantic night I had planned. She was seasick from the rolling swells. I could hear her muttering veiled threats of mutiny and something about shark bait. I dropped an anchor, but it did not want to hold, and the broken boat kept up a continuous banging against the hull. Finally, in

the early morning, a passing powerboat gave us a hand to cut
the dingy and rope loose. Not too much was said on the
return trip home. The *Fantasy*, on that leg of the journey, had
lost its magic.

There was one last sailing excursion for me and the dark-
eyed girl before we became like ships in the night. We had
one week left in the Irish Rover tour of Australia. The final
engagement was to be performed at the opening of a very
exclusive tennis club. We were staying in the flashy suites on
the beach, and just a short distance away I noticed some small
catamarans for day-sailing rentals. "I don't want to go sailing,"
she moaned. "I'm still getting over that night in Melbourne.
Forget it!"

"Ah, ca-man," I mimicked. "It'll be great fun just for an hour.
What do ya say—huh, huh, huh?" I joked, hoping she would
say yes.

"Look!" (She always started with a command of look! when
she was trying to explain things angrily to me.) "I'll just end up
in the water with you. I went to the hairdresser's this morning
and tonight is that special tennis club affair. I just want to
relax and do my nails, so piss off, mate!" (Aussie women have
a fine convict colonial command of the Queen's English.)

"No, no, no!" I insisted. "You'll love these little boats. I can
sail them with my eyes closed. They go like surfboards and
you'll be glad you came."

Against her wishes she climbed aboard the sailboat. A
piece of heavy canvas was stretched between the two hulls,
and I prepared for a rollicking sail along the shore. It was
difficult taking off from a sandy beach, and as soon as I
hoisted the mainsail the thing took off in a real gust of wind.
I barely had time to jump aboard. The lady started cursing
immediately as the spray splashed all over her new hairdo.
Her grumblings grew as we churned away down the beach in

an ever more boisterous breeze. "Jeeze-us! I want off," I heard her yell. "Slow this bloody thing down! I don't want to go out any further, barrrstard! I'm getting soaked." For some demented reason I couldn't help roaring with laughter.

I could hear a whistle now in the sail and the waves were splashing over the deck. Her hairdo was seaweed and my jollity subsided somewhat as I realized I couldn't handle this clumsy tourist boat. As the beach grew more distant behind, she screamed an order for me to turn around and head back to shore. Always ready to please, I whipped the rudder into a tack and the little "cat" tipped up first on one hull. Then both hulls did a lovely flip—upside down in the surf.

As the snarling female lashed out in her best Australian crawl for the beach, true to nautical tradition, I refused to leave the ship. I truthfully didn't want to swim in those shark-infested bays, or pay for a lost rental boat. So I hung on to the upturned hulls, struggling to climb up on top to keep the Irish legs out of the water. Those pictures of shark attacks are enough to make me afraid to use the shower on the Australian beaches, never mind swim a quarter mile out to sea.

In the crystalline water I could see the mast pointing toward the sea bottom, and honest to God I swear I saw a giant shadow pass below. My suntanned deserter, who was now just climbing out of the surf and shaking her fist at me, was heading back to the hotel room without a second whimsical thought that perhaps she should send some of those lifeguards with the rope belts and funny beanie hats out after me.

I thought with horror about her brother who had made the front page of the local paper a few months earlier. The picture showed him posing on the beach with half a surfboard, which had been ripped apart by a jagged cut received while riding in on the board. Something huge had mistaken him for a giant spoon bait lure and had taken a great frenzied gulp of that heavy fiberglass board, sending him flying up in the air.

"Oh, Mother!" I thought in a panic. "Why do I never learn to stay in the pubs along the wharves of the world? Why do I have this need to play sea captain?" I bobbed along for a mile or so from the rental dock and, to my relief, the mast struck bottom. Then it was bump and shudder as I bounced along in the swells just beyond the breaking waves. It was like riding a big pogo stick. Unfortunately I was drifting closer to shore and soon I would get picked up by the surf. My landing would be at a busy part of the beach and it was full of sunbathers, who were starting to watch my embarrassing arrival.

I am always conscious of not looking like a fool at the helm and so I slipped into my habit of role-playing, which always seems to take a hold of me in times of trouble and stress. (My mother once threatened to have me committed if I didn't stop doing Laurel and Hardy and saying, "Another fine mess you've got us into!" and "It certainly is, Ollie" every time she was telling me off.) Now I was wondering if I could jettison the main mast and pretend I was on a large surfboard, the latest twin-hull surfboard. Mind you, my Irish tweed seaman's cap, which I usually wear at sea, and my long, oversized, khaki T-shirt to protect myself from any more sunburn, would likely be a dead giveaway that I was not a real surfer.

A couple of German tourists swimming out in the surf paddled up to my upturned craft, "Ya need some help, ya?"

"Nein, danke!" I waved nonchalantly as they body-surfed back to shore. "Nein, danke," I repeated, quite pleased with my German. "Ach dhu liber! Mein shatz!" I said in my best Hitleresque, as the catamaran got lifted up on the back of a long wave and tumbled to the beach.

Suddenly I transformed into a torpedoed U-boat captain as played by Laurel and Hardy and I was wondering how to say,

"another fine mess," in German. I slipped off the back of my
submarine into the water and staggered ashore. I pulled my
cap low over my ears and with the long khaki shirt down to my
knees, I dragged the life jacket behind me along the beach. I
mumbled German apologies to all the sunbaked people oiling
their skins as I sloshed water on bikinis and hairy tanned
muscles.

"Ach, mein Gott! Such a war!" I mumbled, as I threaded my
way amongst them heading back to my own lines. They
probably saw through my disguise and pointed at me with
covert whispers. "Look there Sheila, see that strange little
Irish-looking person. He's dressed for the North Sea for God
sake and leaving that sailboat capsized in the surf—Pommie
tourist barrstards," they seemed to be yelling at me. So I
switched to their own mother tongue. "Good as gold, mates—
she'll be right!" I yelled, just to make them less suspicious.

That little escapade cost me plenty, and the rental people
charged me both for damage and to have "Das Boat" brought
to its moorage, for it ended up a mile and a half away with the
aluminum mast stuck in the sand and bent almost in two with
the surf. It was also the last time my sailing partner would ever
venture out with me again—even though I did arrange for a
handsome hairdresser to come to the room and redo her
seaweed hair.

That night on stage I was in agony with my sunburned face
and legs, and looked like a lobster, as I painfully tried to
entertain all the glittering people who had paid five hundred
dollars a plate for the charity dinner. The charity should have
been to send this Laurel and Hardy red boy to sailing camp for
deranged sailors.

Before long the sun set in an Aussie blaze over the
Melbourne coast as well as on that relationship. I vowed to all
the sirens of the deep that I would become a landsman. I

wouldn't even have a pond or an inflatable pool. I'd give up painting any more of my little marine scenes of my favorite ships. No more would I play the wild sailing rover, no more! Of course the other sea person in me bought books of plans for sailboats and started hanging around marinas and making covert plans for building a new motor sailer from stem to stern, living aboard, and sailing off to my postage stamp world.

But with a busy year ahead of Irish Rover touring, I had to settle on building tiny ships in bottles, just to keep myself busy on the road. The music was in popular demand, which meant months spent in hotel rooms. I relieved the boredom by this time-gobbling pastime and sent the ships in a bottle off to friends and relatives with words of wishful thinking.

Aboard
Fantasy in
Melbourne

She's flying before a North Sea gale
or maybe she's rounding The Horn.
She's running spices from the East
To arrive on Christmas morn.
She's the good ship Irish Rover
Slicing through the wave.
Made from the wreck on many a beach
I carried home to save.
Now dear friend you're in charge
You're the captain and the crew.
The charts and logs and fancy
I leave them all to you.
If there's a time when worries have left you dry ashore
Hoist her sails and anchor, leave your own front door.
Head her south to the Indies or north to the Arctic Sea
For a ship that's in a bottle sails the heart to where it's free.

—Bodega Bay, California

SEVENTH VERSE

Missionary dreams and friendly harbors

*I*n the Maritime Museum in San Francisco there is a
seventeen-foot sloop on display called *The Mermaid*.
Kinichi Horie, a young Japanese sailor, sailed it across
the vast Pacific from Japan and it now sits in exactly the same
condition as when he arrived. I've examined that little cabin,
with all his gear spread around. I experience a twinge of fear
just thinking about that voyage alone in those wild seas, or is
it envy that I feel? It makes me wonder what drives these souls
who have the courage to face death at sea. I believe we all
respect these adventurers who dare to push themselves
beyond that comfort zone where we all try to confine our
souls.

I suppose I feel strangely frustrated that I could never
duplicate that feat for my life seems to have always had its
confines and even its comfort zones. There was a good living
to be made in the music business, and somehow most of my
time was spent touring, with four other crew members to
consider as well as a whole support gang. All I could do was
dream of voyages of adventure and an escape from the endless
years as a traveling musician. I think we all have a sailor soul
inside that calls us to be free, but only a very few can abandon

everything and, like that lone Japanese youth, set out on the one great adventure of life.

After my mishaps in Australia I swore to those sirens of the deep that I would stay off the water, and of course I lied to the seductive nude lady creatures with the fishy tales. They crooned a new tune to me out there in their watery boudoir, and, like a drunken skipper, I whistled into the sea wind, which, as any old salt knows, is a most unlucky thing to do. They heard me, smiled a seaweedy grin, and waited. I ordered a Chinese junk from a Hong Kong shipyard, and it got damaged on the freighter en route to Canada when it tipped off its cradle. I lost my deposit and never did take command of that exotic wooden boat.

A couple of years would race by as I played my music across the world, and the portals were open to all those places of my childhood dreams. I rented sailing boats here and there around the globe and I grabbed all the joy I could find. Somehow those sirens lured me into some highly satisfying seas: I have felt the warm indigo ocean off the coast of Tahiti in a big trimaran cutting through that living South Pacific. I have played my Irish jigs to a sake-slurping captain of a Japanese boat that I tried sailing off the coast of Japan, all the while thinking of the young Japanese sailor heading out into the Pacific for San Francisco and immortality in the marine museum.

What exactly is the madness that grabs hold of a man's sanity and makes him want to put to sea or lake or millpond in any old thing that floats? I say man without being sexist for I have met some world-class women sailors who make boats their life. Somehow they are not truly driven to be afloat in the same way as men. Women appear to me to be less romantic and more practical about the art.

Check out any marina on a weekend, and the contented

souls you encounter messing about the multitude of assorted floating things will be about ninety percent men. They make weekend widows of their wives as they head off for the day with a car full of tools, paint, wire and rope, coolers full of beer, bait, and soggy sandwiches, fishing tackle, radio equipment, magazines, and perhaps the next great unfinished novel of their future sailing adventures. How often I've heard them tell me that in three or four years they plan to pack up the entire family, build or buy a bigger steel-hulled vessel, and sail off with the tide to tranquil oceans and uncomplicated pleasures and home schooling.

I envy those adventuresome few who actually follow through with their offshore sailing plans. I will seek them out at yacht club parties like a hypochondriac homing in on a doctor, and they will find me a hungry listener for I feel at home with these boat scrapers and hull painters, the knot tiers, barnacle bashers, and wind worshippers who congregate around the shambles of docks and sheds. I am a soul mate to these hardy few who live in cluttered, mildewy cabins full of glorious confusion. Think of all the millions of hours spent messing about in boats, then think of the minuscule number of nautical miles actually traveled, and you will get an idea of the most perfect way to waste time ever dreamed up by mankind.

Ah yes, I must go down to the sea again, and all I ask is a tall ship, a luxury ship, a great big mother-of-all ships, bigger than the *Titanic* and the *Edmund Fitzgerald*. Those two were not supposed to sink. Expert seamanship and reinforced hulls are no match against Neptune's outbursts of anger. In the wind I could often hear his scornful bellows. "You puny, drownable landlubber. What gall! To face my tempestuous wrath with your flimsy craft and weekend seaman's knowledge. Stand to, till I blow you a watery kiss that'll send you to Hades."

The years rattled and hummed with Irish music, and I settled on the West Coast of Canada in Vancouver. Then came a successful television show beaming across the country every Sunday night for years, and the Irish Rovers became a big part of the Canadian entertainment scene. Like a sailor in every port, I found some short love affairs with summer girls and with old boats, the two things that ever moved me to my peak. I discovered a magnificent yacht called the *Blackhawk Two*, a real beauty moored in Lake Winnipeg and going for a very affordable price. I was a spendthrift in those days and my savings were always very thin. But I had a house that I could sell and I decided the time had come to live aboard a boat at last. I found a moorage in Vancouver and then realized I needed to find a way to move this fifty-foot beauty from Lake Winnipeg to the sea coast in Vancouver!

Now if you look at a map of central Canada, you will find that there are not many canals or waterways out of the prairies. The boat was too big to travel by trailer so I struck on an idea that was so preposterous everyone loved it. I tried to talk the Goodyear blimp people into airlifting the boat over the Rockies in sections—just for the PR value. The boatbuilder told me he could reassemble the *Blackhawk* in Vancouver, and my mind worked overtime trying to visualize boat sections floating down the western slope to the marina by Stanley Park in Vancouver. Well, the great airlift never took place, and I had to forget the *Blackhawk* and settle on some floating houseboat in Sausalito for a short while.

Houseboat living was not all I thought it would be, so I became an apartment dweller on English Bay in Vancouver's west end. From my window I could watch the big tankers come and go from distant shores. Hundreds of sailboats dotted the bay all year round, and you don't need to own a sailboat in Vancouver if you have friends. So, contented enough, I was taken aboard other people's boats and waited for the next harbor to call me.

A year went by in that crowded environment and home was the sailor, home from the discontented sea with no more red sails in the sunset or half-drowned rosy daydreams. I grew more unsettled and restless by the week and was relieved whenever the next Irish Rover tour commenced.

I found myself always watching hopefully for that one soul who was destined to share my dreams. When the dark-eyed Australian girl ran out of spiritual boomerangs and there was nothing left to return, I drifted into a long space of waiting— for what I wasn't sure. In my heart I longed for a safe harbor for I was tired of the party music and dreamed about a small house by the sea on some friendly shore. I was waiting for someone I had dreamed about and I knew she was there. I could feel her peaceful presence amid all the noise, a woman who would be my confidante and who had children in her eyes. I even imagined that she would love me for all my misadventures through life.

Then it happened, all in one wonderful summer of 1976. Early in the year I had tried some yoga breathing and meditation. The other boys in the band would make fun of my messing around with the Maharishi, but we had after all journeyed through the Haight-Ashbury era in San Francisco and I had known people who had achieved some real results from meditation. I thought perhaps I could elevate my mind to a peaceful plane and meditate on sailing across vast uncharted oceans.

One quiet afternoon after months of trying, I felt a great wave of peace swirl around me and I achieved a feeling of floating. It seemed that I almost stopped breathing just to keep the journey moving. I felt I was flying high above the ocean and across wide hillsides covered in pine trees, and I experienced my first in a series of lucid dreamlike scenes. Sometimes in my half-asleep state I would find myself in a tropical place. I could hear the surf, and the subtle aroma of perfumed flowers would drift over my senses. I would come to a white colonial church and then a green-roofed house where there was a beautiful, gentle woman in a room that seemed familiar to me.

It was all so clear and real, yet I was aware that I was having a waking dream and knew that I was only an onlooker in this other space and time. The room was dressed in the Victorian period, and the girl with the golden hair tied up in a bun was in love with me. I could feel it, and I was full of a certain sadness because I knew that when I awoke she would disappear. She was the daughter of a missionary and the place was Hilo on the island of Hawaii sometime in the 1870s. I was the first mate on a whaling ship and my name was Matthew Anderson. I was wild and fresh in from the sea when I met the missionary's daughter in my dream.

At this point I had never been to Hawaii except for stopovers en route to Australia. The first time I experienced this dream, I was amazed at every clear picture. I sat in the kitchen while the girl worked at the table; I saw her face and every detail of the room right down to the vegetables she was preparing. I talked to her and told her about the future, about flying machines that would carry

Playing the part of Matthew Anderson

people above the clouds to these islands in a matter of hours. She laughed a merry laugh and told me I was "touched" by the heat.

At the end of the first dream, I remember introducing myself to her father who had come in and told me to be on my way before dark. Then a large horse was rearing up and kicking in the yard and her father said, "Look there, boy, get that horse in control and put him away. The wind is rising and the horse is nervous." As I reached the door and grasped the brass knob I paused because I knew that when I left the room all would be gone. Just then a gust of wind grabbed the door and slammed it. When I turned back to the room all was indeed gone and I found myself back on my couch, feeling an overwhelming sense of loss, wondering what happened to Matthew Anderson and the missionary's child.

The story did not end there in some distant time in Hilo. Fate opened a doorway and I decided I would go to Hawaii to stay with my old friends Bud and June Dant, soul mates from our Decca recording days in Los Angeles. Bud recorded our first hit, "The Unicorn," and we have remained close ever since. He is a living legacy of the Jazz age and great fun to be with. He and his wife were retired from the mad Hollywood music scene and living a spiritual life on the "Big" Island. When they invited me to come for a visit, I jumped at the chance for the winter had been long and dreary, and my soul needed some solace and color. Being a lone bachelor it was easy to head off for the sun while all the other Rovers went home to loving children and wives.

There in the Vancouver airport, as I sat watching the endless stream of strangers hurrying in all directions, I noticed a girl who seemed familiar to me. The feeling was so strong I had the impulse to go over to her and say "Hello, remember me?" She appeared to be waiting for someone and I could not take my eyes off her. When I saw the familiar way she moved as she flicked her long golden hair back and tied it in a bun, it brought back my Hawaiian dream. She was wearing white and a peaceful air seemed to surround her amid all of the airport noise. I took out my diary and wrote: "I think I have just discovered the missionary's daughter! She is real and she looks kind and beautiful. Oh God, how can I meet her!"

When I looked up from the page she was gone. I quickly scanned the whole area, but there was no sign of her. She had vanished like my waking dream, and I wondered if I had simply transferred the face of that girl in the dream onto some stranger. I quickly packed up my diary and satchel and walked around to see if I could catch one more glimpse of the summer girl in white. I felt that same sense of loss that had touched me when I woke from the lucid dream.

I made my way to the departure lounge when they announced the last boarding call and there she was, as fate would have it, traveling on the same flight. I tried not to make it too obvious that I was staring, but I could not take my eyes from her as she sat reading a book. I wanted to ask her if her father was a missionary. I wanted her to know me, like I felt I knew her. She looked up from the book toward me, and for an instant our eyes met. I felt a great wave of my energy flow all around her in that instant like a warm globe of golden warmth. I believe we all have a human energy field around our being and how wonderful it would be if we could control it and send out only good and loving waves.

My energy field was certainly crackling and glowing on that day with a hundred years of lost love. What happened next was another in a series of fateful events, and I could hardly believe my good fortune when into the waiting room came the happy, friendly face of an old sweetheart of mine from the airline business called Leanne. She did not see me at first and went over and sat beside the mysterious girl in the white dress. They were traveling together, and I noticed both were carrying airline bags.

When Leanne spotted me she came over with her cheery smile and gave me a hug. We shared some catching-up chitchat as the passengers started trooping aboard. I whispered to her, "Who's the girl you're traveling with? I want to meet her."

"Don't bother," she said. "Her name is Cathy and she is just getting over a love affair. I don't think she'll be interested, but come on." I strode across the waiting room in my best manly gait dressed in my tropical bush shirt and swinging my leather satchel. Just as I was about to shake her hand I walloped a large chrome ashtray with the swinging satchel and sent it crashing across the marble floor with a God almighty racket and a spraying of sand and cigarette butts. Everyone in the place was startled, and as I kneeled down to pick up the mess, my satchel spilled open and all the glorious junk from my travels scattered onto the floor as well.

It was not the perfect introduction that I wanted for Matthew Anderson—my other ego. She shook my hand and her blue eyes were smiling in amusement at my confused grand

Catherine, the missionary's daughter

entrance. I discovered that instead of being a missionary's child she was with the airlines and by chance was being flown with a whole flight crew to Hawaii to wait out a strike. I invited the two girls to come and visit me on the Big Island if they got tired of Waikiki, and the lady thanked me and smiled.

I talked with Leanne and her new boyfriend during the flight, and every so often I would feel the blue eyes of that girl in the white dress glance over the book she was reading and smile at me. I disembarked and rushed off the plane to buy a flower lei for her and Leanne as they came out with their luggage. "I have a nice little place in Kona right on the beach. You're welcome to come and stay," I told them once more, perhaps a little too anxiously since it was a lie. I was of course staying with my old record producer Bud Dant.

I never really thought that it would happen but a call came to Bud's house that night from Leanne and I was caught. "Can we come over and stay with you? This place is dreadful," she said. I spluttered and stammered and said, "Great! I'll pick you up at the airport in Kona tomorrow evening." I was a man possessed, racing around to every real estate rental office I could find. I spent all that evening searching and by some lucky chance found a small cottage right on the beach, just as I had told them.

My old friend came with her boyfriend and another couple. Catherine, for that's what seemed right for me to call her, was still getting over her love affair at home and was traveling alone. "Thank you, St. Anthony," I whispered to the horizon. For one week we all lived together, and I spent hours sharing my thoughts with her. Bud was leading the Kona palace band at the King Kamehameha Ball to celebrate the 1776 bicentennial, and he had given me two tickets. I was full of a high joy when Catherine agreed to come as my guest. That afternoon we went shopping and I helped her pick out a dress for the occasion. (Later we would both agree that we each felt as if we had known each other for years.) It was such an electric time and I was aching with a strange yearning feeling, wondering how I could win her love.

I told her about my dream and she looked down in her quiet way, probably thinking that this was just some well-used line from a strange sailor-musician. All that week we walked and talked. At night we would sit under the giant Hawaiian moon and I was lost in her beauty. It was a passionate setting and one made for love, but there was no more than a gentle touch and a pouring out of my soul. I was just glad to have discovered that sometimes dreams can be real.

EIGHTH VERSE

Home is the sailor

When the Hawaiian trip was over and we parted, I felt as if I would never be the same. She was off to reunite with her old love of three years. It was no consolation when she told me that while he wanted to get engaged she was not sure how she felt anymore about their relationship. I told her honestly that I hoped she would find the happiness she was searching for.

I drove back from the airport after I had waved her and my guests good-bye. The house by the sea had lost all its magic and I felt her presence in every room. I was heartbroken, drowning my nights in rum and music, and soon headed back to my apartment in Vancouver to get ready for yet another tour and television show in the Maritimes. I had been to Nova Scotia quite a few times in the past and I was always glad of a return visit. This would be my first trip to Prince Edward Island and I was looking forward to the change for it might take my mind off the Hawaiian dream. I wanted to call her before I left, but I wasn't sure what I would say.

I stared at the phone for a long time trying to get up the nerve. I expected to hear that she was engaged to be married. My heart was pounding as I finally forced my fingers to dial. As the phone rang and rang, I was almost hoping she wouldn't answer and I'd be spared her kind good-bye. To my elation she sounded happy to hear my voice when she picked up the phone.

"What happened to you? Why didn't you call me earlier?" she asked. "I thought you didn't like me."

"Like you?" I cried. "I think I've loved you for a hundred and fifty years." She laughed at my patter and I tried to be casual when I asked her about the engagement. She told me that she had started going with the young man when they were both only seventeen and she had never known any other love. When she returned and met with him she realized that she wasn't ready to be engaged and perhaps they both needed time to discover where they belonged. I told her that I couldn't wait to see her again. "Catherine, my dear woman," I said, "I suppose I couldn't talk you into a visit to Prince Edward Island? I'll be there for a week taping a TV show and I might get a boat and take you sailing."

"I'd love to go sailing with you, sailor," she said and laughed in that merry way that seemed so familiar. (At this point she knew nothing of my sailing prowess.) "I've loved P.E.I. ever since I went camping there as a young girl with my family. I'll try to get a pass on the flight to Halifax and I'll take you out for lobster. Can you put up with me for a couple of days?"

"How about a couple of centuries," I thought to myself, but I didn't want to scare her away. When I hung up the phone I went strutting around the house like first mate Matthew Anderson and I did a couple of jumps over the coffee table. "Way-hey and up she rises," I sang at the top of my lungs as I made plans for my visit to the old Island of St. John, now called P.E.I.

The "Island" lies across the Northumberland Strait from Nova Scotia, and at that time a ferry at Cape Tormentine in neighboring New Brunswick sailed you across to one of the most beautiful summer places in all of Canada. Catherine met me in Halifax and as we drove through the warm countryside, I was enthralled by her gentle beauty. We certainly seemed like old acquaintances and on that bright summer day our life together started. As she stood beside me on the ferry I was happier than at any other time I could remember. The red clay banks and the old whitewashed lighthouses greeted us and said to me, "Come in from away and stop a while." She seemed to belong to this place, she had the aroma of fresh soap and wildflowers, and her hair shone in the sunlight. There was a warm seductive wind coming from the south and if I could, I would have pushed a button to stop the moment.

This was the beginning of a whole new and wonderful part of my life's voyage for Catherine was destined to become my dear companion and the mother of a "full-blown crew," of three little shipmates for all my future sailings. I believe in magic these days and I believe in sailing. The dream that I had before I met Catherine was lucid and real, and I sat down and wrote this dream song the day that she came to me in Hawaii. I called it "Missionary's Child." The words came out all in one flow of thought and it was recorded on my favorite Irish Rover album, *Tall Ships and Salty Dogs*. It may not be the perfect gentle love song, but it captured the excitement of the time.

> *My name is Matthew Anderson and I come from the Boston Town,*
> *I sailed on a Yankee whaling ship to the southern whaling ground.*
> *It was my first trip on a whaling ship and the life was hard to bear*
> *But I heard about the girls in Hilo town and the whale-fish everywhere.*
>
> *When I got down into Hilo town all that they said was true,*
> *Our ship was full of oil me boys, there was girls for all the crew.*
> *But I fell in with a Yankee maid, from Maryland she came.*
> *Her father was a missionary, that's what she said, and she was just the*
> *   same.*

Chorus: *Way-hey roll and go—hide your daughters down below.*
There's a Yankee ship out in the bay
and we're coming to town for some fun today.

Before I had a chance to run she had taken me by the hand,
She led me down to her daddy's church down by the Hilo strand.
Instead of rolling up in bed with some dark-eyed Hilo whore
I sang the hymns and yelled Amen! with the maid from Baltimore.

So now my whaling's over, my sailing days are done
Those big blue eyes of the Yankee maid spoiled a sailor's fun.
But she taught me how to sing and preach, she loved me up and down
So here I'll stay with the missionary's child in that sunny Hilo town.

Prince Edward Island had a seduction all planned for me. The weather had stayed hot all month, and the steely blue ocean and red sandy shoreline drew me into the escape spell that so many visitors feel on that summer island. Catherine and I drove the country roads for the few short days we were together, and I was sad to have to say good-bye as she flew off to the world. But with her promise to meet me in Vancouver, I happily set about my music business for I knew that this time there would be more summer days ahead for us.

The net was cast. I was high on the thought of Catherine, the Island was part of that charm, and I was drawn to its seashores. Perhaps it was an impossible dream, but somehow I wanted to live on this distant island and just maybe the missionary's child would come and share this sailor's dream.

Looking back now on the chain of events it feels as though it was all a grand master plan. I was being directed by powers beyond my comprehension, and I have often said a silent prayer of thanks for that wonderful period of my life. From the first moment, I was moved to be a part of that place of small

harbors, fishing boats, and Maritime history. Catherine had
set the spell in motion, and my feelings were high that fine
summer night when I was invited to a fiddle party that would
kick off my relationship with the people of that beautiful
island. In the velvet dark night, cool and full of stars, I was
transported from the old Charlottetown Hotel to somewhere
on the eastern shore. They told me that some Cape Breton
fiddlers would be coming and since that didn't really mean
much to me at the time I went along rather reluctantly, hoping
to find a bit of an old Irish "Hooley."

The Calamity Brothers was the unlikely name of the Murphy
brothers' band and they were the ones who had extended the
invitation. Traveling down with me that night was good old
John Allen Cameron, the first man to put the music of Cape
Breton on the map. The other character was Canada's country-
folk poet Stompin' Tom Connors. "By God!" I thought to
myself, "this could be some night!"

We hurtled through the island dark in a packed car full of
rum fumes, and just as I was beginning to regret the wild ride,
we were into the thick of bagpipes, fiddles, and moonshine,
molasses dripping from home-baked biscuits, lobsters by the
bathful and honest-to-God real people. It was an all-night
affair, and I must have told everyone who would listen
about my Hawaiian dream and meeting the lady Catherine
(undoubtedly they thought it was the moonshine working
its alchemy on this musical Irishman).

I woke up in the morning in Gerard Murphy's home
surrounded by a gang of children. The bacon was sizzling in
Karen Murphy's kitchen and the kids were singing "The
Unicorn" in honor of their hungover guest. I was "Down Home"
and I only wished that Catherine had been able to stay. I'm
sure that with her Scottish traditions she would have felt right
at home since she grew up learning to do the Highland fling

from her mother while her grandfather played tunes from his native Orkney on the fiddle.

I asked Gerard Murphy, my new musical friend, if he would take me around the seashore, with the idea of finding a likely place to rent for the rest of summer or possibly buy if the price was right. He was happy to oblige for he was an Islander through and through. He knew every nook and cranny and was very proud of his corner of the world. He was a big fellow with an Abraham Lincoln beard and I always thought he looked remarkably like photographs of old Abe. Like Mr. Lincoln, Gerard Murphy was a woodsman and a homespun philosopher and, what's more, an experienced man of the sea for he had spent his childhood fishing lobster with his father. In Ireland there's an old saying: "You can judge your friends by the ones you'd take with you on a lifeboat." I'd certainly take Gerard Murphy aboard.

I was surprised that many of the old farmhouses with nice little acreages could be purchased for less than fifty thousand dollars, a far cry from the rocketing real estate in Toronto or

Gerard Murphy, my good mate in P.E.I.

San Francisco. We looked at quite a few old farms but none of
them felt right until later in the afternoon we took a bumpy
ride through the woods on a shortcut down a red clay road,
heading back to the Murphy house. Thornton Road ended at
the seashore at the mouth of a long inlet, and basking in the
summer sun, across the wide entrance of the Montague River,
was a little town of wooden houses behind an old dock. We
drove on past some whispering aspens and silver birch and
through a field of long grass. It was there that the house
waited at the end of a long overgrown laneway, nestled
between old gnarled hawthorn trees. The first moment I set
eyes on the "Point" and the old Clarke farmhouse, I felt a chill
of excitement and a strong sense of belonging.

The property was surrounded by coral-colored beaches, and
the whole scene reminded me of one of those sunburned
Andrew Wyeth paintings. I stood in the warm wind, staring and
feeling the pull of the magnet of life that was drawing me
toward this old weatherbeaten farmhouse. Gerard pulled a
board off a window and we climbed into the dim, hot, and
dusty room. The heart of the place started to pulse, and the
house seemed to come alive as we opened more shutters to
let in the sunlight. Threads of future memories like silver
cobwebs were starting to spin that would later be woven into
a grand patchwork of life around the wooden house on St.
Andrew's Point.

Estate agents and distant owners were tracked down, and
then the usual problems with finances and practical reasoning
reared their ugly heads. If I had allowed any one of those
sensible emotions to take control of my impulses, many
fateful roads would have changed directions. I've never let
reason get in the way of a head full of daydreams! Perhaps I
should have done so now and then, but not this time. I was
driven by an energy that wouldn't let go. Waiting for me,

behind those tattered walls of peeling wallpaper, were love and children and old boats and stories. By God, I'd have a chunk of that and with the powers of fate on my side who could stop me!

As we rattled round the Island that week I told all my Irish tales to the Murphy brothers, Gerard and Gene, and to all the other goodly company who made me a part of their life and shared the yarns of my rovings and ravings. I was well known in those days in Canada from the weekly Irish Rovers TV show, but the Murphys didn't care about that. It didn't matter who you were as long as you were willing to be their friend.

Well, as the old expression goes, "A bird never flew on one wing." I found another wing in me Da. He offered to travel out to the Island in the late fall to try to get the old house livable. Looking back on it all now, I realize it was quite a sacrifice to journey from my mother's cozy life to the edge of winter and take up residence alone in a drafty, century-old farm dwelling hidden away at the bottom of a clay road at the end of an island in the Gulf of St. Lawrence.

He settled in with amazing frontiersmanship and soon a new iron stove was spreading its pleasant heat to frozen corners of the house. No more cracking the ice off the dog's water dish. When Da got his melodeon de-iced he soon had the old walls jumping, and the setter and the wee music man settled happy as you please. That red dog raced joyfully for miles along empty beaches, a mad companion for my father.

Once again my father's music brought him friends, and Gerard was happy to have Bob join The Calamity Brothers. "By jeepers," Da would exclaim to me on the phone, "we sound bloody good." Soon his jigs and reels were jumping around the Island, and he was having the time of his life.

That winter was wild! "Never experienced anything like it," he said shivering to me on the weekly phone calls. He told me

*Wee Bob
happy on
the Island
with me*

I was crazy to even think of living down there in the winter
months. Everyone I met outside the Island told me the same
thing when I told them I was in the process of moving out
there full time. Oh there were many times I too had my
doubts, but "Wee Bob's" unflagging spirit made it possible for
me to move the following spring. By that time the house was
warm and ready for all my adventures.

Somehow, and to this day I am still amazed and grateful,
Catherine joined me in that Island farmhouse. With her quiet
inspiration and house-making arts, she turned the 1861 farm
and lighthouse into a delightful place to live. (We later
acquired a vintage 1860 lighthouse from the town of Montague
and towed it through the fields to be attached to the house.)
The editors of *Home Decor Canada* magazine featured her work
in a colorful article on country living.

At last I had my "Captain's House," and my missionary's
daughter made the place sing. My father stayed with us the
first year and we were glad of his company and his handy way

You want to do what? Move a lighthouse?!

The house on St. Andrew's Point with the lighthouse attached.

with house construction. There was never any friction with his presence in our home, and Catherine and my Da had many good conversations over a bottle of wine. We settled into Island life as if we had both expected it all to happen.

When I read through my diaries of that first year, there comes floating out of the salty pages a sailpast of memories.

Page from An Island Diary

The red clay road is buried in drifts of sparkling snow, silent now and peaceful after an April storm raged on the eastern end of the Island for the last two nights. The blizzard howled across Cape Breton with the fury that you'd expect from mid-January gales, but this morning all is forgiven, the road and the seaside woods are at last ready for spring.

I've spent a good deal of time in winter woods

and have grown familiar with the sounds of solitude. One day you realize with a certain joy that the hidden places are teeming with life and sound. Small invisible birds somehow survive in these woods of frozen spruce; fox, rabbit, and a multitude of furry creatures blaze trails, making little pathways through the marshmallow snow between the trees. When April comes and winter retreats, the solitude starts to crack and hum. There is a subtle tonal change in the song of the chickadee: "I made it!" says the tune. "Another spring to build."

The perfect stillness amplifies when I leave the road and follow an old farm laneway down toward the sea. There's a ruined foundation deep in Thornton Woods, made from hand-hewn blocks of reddish sandstone placed there over a hundred years earlier. Fiddle music filled the glade here long ago, and the wild laughter of children brightened the air. Only the chickadee and I think about them this morning. There seems to be a ghostly echo left lingering in the burned beams and tumbled stones. Below the pine branches the snow is pure and its taste reminds me of Irish spring water and that childhood far away. On the edge of the frozen beach, small streams are already gurgling under the ice into the bay. The rocks that stretch out a bony hand from the Graveyard Point are alive with lumpy seals and their song of groan and croak echoes along the shore. Like me they rejoice in the white spring morning. The gulls and a kingfisher lift my spirit, full of memories of that first introduction to "The Island" only a few rushing months ago.

—April 1977

The ancient mariner and me

O ut of the mists over the Montague River came a man like a ghost from the past, a character I am sure I will never forget. Sometimes, when I am far away and feeling down, I resurrect the man, and his comings and goings in my mind will give me a lift and a smile. He was the original ancient mariner and his name was George Vatcher. "You'll have to meet this boy," my Da had said with a laugh. "He wants to swap my button-key accordion for a lobster boat." Say no more! Down I went to meet this mad trader.

A mile or so from our windswept farmhouse was a garbage dump where I had dropped off a few packing cases and an old chair a week earlier. Now my father

"Captain" George Vatcher

escorted me to the edge of this trash heap. "This is where he lives," my Da announced with grandeur.

"He lives in the dump?" I asked.

"It's not the real dump," he assured me with little conviction. "There's a wee cabin away up the back there." I tramped over rubble from wrecked houses, stepped over the skulls and bones of cattle, and negotiated broken lobster traps and piles of old appliances.

George Vatcher was a collector of glorious trash. Two or three decrepit wooden boats blocked the pathway, and as I was clambering over one of them, a bellow and a tuneless song erupted from the direction of the small cabin. "Here comes little Willie, he's a good little man, he plays the banjo in the Irish band." Then out of the door of the cabin, with a flurry and a scattering of ducks and hens, jumped a wild apparition. He was about six foot three and wore a sea captain's hat stuck at a jaunty angle on top of a pile of black, unwashed curls. A tattered greatcoat from some unknown war was draped over his long frame, and a pair of dirty bare feet performed a little island stepdance.

I had never laid eyes on a more magnificent pair of size fourteen, long-toed dirty feet in my whole life. "He could be a great swimmer with flippers like that," I reasoned to myself, almost bursting into laughter. At first glance, George's face looked well tanned, but you soon realized that it hadn't seen soap for a couple of years. Dirt was caked in the washboard surface. (I was amazed later to hear that he was only forty-five years of age.)

He reached out a great paw, mashed my hand, and encased me in a wild, smothering, aromatic hug. The odor that emanated from him reminded me of the zoo. It was human animal scent, the kind that clings to you and your clothing after an encounter with the king of the Lower Montague dump.

The wrinkled grooves of grime on his medieval countenance
let go into a huge toothless laugh (well, almost toothless;
there were three or four black pegs in his mouth), and the
whole smile was reminiscent of a grate in a fireplace.

He roared with grand exuberance, "Did-ja like me song for
ye, dear? I made her up." He then stood back from me and,
holding his arms outstretched, asked straightforwardly, "Well,
how did ye like meetin' me, dear?"

"Ah, it was a rare experience, George," I answered honestly,
with a laugh. Now and then to this day I sometimes get the
urge to repeat George Vatcher's important question at some
highfalutin event, being introduced to some VIP. After the first
thirty seconds of small talk I'd dearly love to announce, "Well,
how did ye like meeting me, dear?" Men do get quite uneasy
when you call them dear or darling. But George called
everyone by these endearments—men, women, and children.

In a city environment, people might be inclined to call
George an old wino, or a derelict. You might even be tempted
to remark, like some of the local fishermen, that he was "one
brick short of a load." Somehow, though, there in his own
unholy space, he was a man of the sea, independent and
timeless, even quite charming and crafty when the need arose.

I learned a lot about life from living on the Island. I learned
not to be too quick to judge people, especially on the first
meeting. My first impression of that weird and wondrous
George was that he was a real old sea dog. His appearance
told me that tall ships were his birthright, and I looked forward
to hearing his store of gigantic sea sagas. Well, his stories
were indeed huge. But as a sailor I have to say he was a life
member of my club. He should have been lost at sea years
earlier because the floating things that he climbed aboard
made my early vessels look like the Onassis yacht.

The lobster boat George had offered to my father in

exchange for his accordion was called the North Star, and it had seen better days and nights. I'm sure she caught her last lobster forty years earlier. The wreck was now lying high and dry under huge piles of rubbish, and I reckon the accordion was the better part of that deal. Anyone, it seemed, who wanted rid of an old scrap boat could just drop it off in Vatcher's Sargasso Sea of junk. There were bottomless bathtubs, dinged-in dingies, and sideless skiffs, along with broken oars and dilapidated dories all piled in glorious confusion. He tinkered away his few sober hours repairing these worthless vessels and rusted outboard engines. Then when he had a good "slap" of gin roaring in his head, he'd risk life and limb putting out to sea in one of his creations. When he wasn't working like a demon with his tin can scoop, he would fish for mackerel. The truly amazing thing about George was that he actually caught lots of fish, and he hooked them on the most ridiculous tackle I ever saw.

I was out rowing one evening during one of those rare Canadian Maritime sunsets of reds and golds that never cease to exult the spirit. The breeze was warm and I was thinking that this just might be the most beautiful place in the whole world. A blue heron glided over a perfect millpond ocean when suddenly the sea erupted in a cacophony of splashes. The sound was like surf racing in over a pebble beach or the applause of a big audience. "Mackerel! Thousands and millions," I screamed, almost falling out of the boat. The next day I rushed out to buy tackle and got ready for the catch of the year.

George saw me in town that day buying the gear and convinced me that I needed him as a guide for the fine art of mackerel fishing. So with a good deal of foreboding, I agreed to risk it with Captain George Vatcher. "OK, Captain Ahab," I joked, "I'll go with you, but no booze."

"No dear!" he cried. "I'll be sober as a drunken judge at his own funeral!" He clutched me by the coat and drew me close to his gin fumes. "Listen dear, we'll catch enough of them darlin' little mackerel fishes to salt down for all winter!" I didn't want to break his enthusiasm or appear standoffish for it seemed I was constantly turning down invitations to dine with him and his old father, "Daddy" Eli. It was not that I was being a snob. It was just that I had seen his dogs eating out of the unwashed pot in which he cooked the dinner.

Down the road I went next morning jigging along to a jaunty whistle, armed with my fancy new expensive rod and reel and some flashy lures, full of expectation for the catch. It was a fine morning as I walked along the summer shore between my St. Andrew's Point farmhouse and the piled-up abode of the scarecrow angler. "Look out, you record tuna," I yelled toward the ocean. I thought to myself that with any luck I'd catch a big feed of mackerel as well.

As I came to the junk pile entrance of his cabin I was quite pleased to discover that a bird had built a nest inside the Vatcher mailbox and the mama bird had just hatched some wee chicks. I took this as a contented omen for my future on St. Andrew's Point. Here was a quiet and undisturbed place where no bills or letters from lawyers came to interrupt the peace. How I wish a small bird could build a nest in my busy postbox.

It was never possible to do anything in a simple way when George was around. Right, I thought, we'll row out, catch a few mackerel, say thanks George, and be back home in a couple of hours. Oh dear God, I should have known better. I stumbled over piles of debris and yelled out George's name. The Vatchers kept some strange, mad dogs and I didn't want to tangle with them. My kindly, well-groomed setter had come along for the walk and was putting his mark on all sorts of exotic items in George's yard when all of a sudden his red hackles stood up on end and he took off homeward at a fierce pace. I understood why when the big man opened the cabin door.

Twelve mongrels of every size, temperament, and mange came tearing toward me through the rubble. The hounds of hell were loose and they were heading in my direction. George began yelling obscenities and hurling bits of firewood at them from his endless supply piled up by the door. Some of his missiles came dangerously close to my head. The dogs, now in full cry, were paying not the least bit of attention to their master's war whoops. One of the smallest and obviously the most aggressive of the pack grabbed me by the back of my jeans. "If one of them touches ye dear, I'll kill the lot o' them!" yelled George in a fury.

"Well, George, my dear, you'd better start killing!" I yelled back at him. "There's one tearing the arse out of my trousers at this very moment." George whacked out with a stick at my small attacker and it let go, yelping its demented head off. The rest joined in on the racket, and those with tails tucked them between their legs, scurrying and skulking back to the cabin.

"Go down to the shore there, dear," he bellowed. "Pull my boat out and I'll be there in a minute." The old wooden dory was made of heavy overlapping planks painted green and was lodged in the bushes. No matter how hard I tugged, I was unable to get it to move more than a foot. George arrived with a galvanized tub and a can of motor oil.

"Where's your fishing gear?" I asked.

"Well," he answered quite nonchalantly, "it's there in the boat, dear. Come on, I'll help ya pull 'er out to the water." The two of us pulled and heaved but it wouldn't budge an inch! George started scooping fistfuls of sand out of the boat with his shovel-like hands.

Old Daddy Eli had stumbled down the path to watch the fishermen set out to sea and he stood there grinning, inspecting our efforts. "Can you not give us a bit of a pull, Daddy!" yelled George in frustration.

"Nope," said Eli, "but I'll do you one better. I'll untie the rope that's tied to the bush." Both of us looked at Eli in disbelief as he fumbled in the bushes and tossed out the end of the rope. "Yer a smart little man, Daddy," grinned George, hammering the old veteran of the Great War on the back.

Eli, a frail skin-and-bones kind of man, staggered and sprawled flat on the sand from the blow. When he regained his feet, he took a wild swipe at his son, spitting a mouthful of sand at his daft offspring. George dragged a rusty outboard and an equally rusty gasoline can from the bushes and started splashing dirty-looking fuel into the engine. A cigarette dangled from his cracked lips like a fuse, close to the gasoline. Eli and I moved quickly and nimbly back a safe fifty feet, and the old man's face contorted into a fiendishly toothless grin. "Ye eejit," he yelled, "I hope you blow yer'sel to Newfoundland where I found ya."

God protects his strange creatures, and before long the wooden boat was in the water, ready to sail, at least that's what I thought. Unfortunately, a small fountain was bubbling up through a hole between the planks. George took a piece of driftwood

Cork 'er, and maybe she'll float.

and cut a rounded point, prodded it into the leak, then smashed it a good blow with a stone. This rather ingenious bung seemed to work and reluctantly I waded in and climbed aboard the dory he called the *Luxury Lady*. "Okay, George, I give up, you've got me. Where's your fishing tackle?" There was not a thing aboard belonging to him that even resembled fishing gear.

Without answering he handed me a small penknife, then told me to reach under the seat. I discovered a huge ball of tangled fishing line and, following his directions, cut and tied dozens of short lengths together. Soon George was ready to fish. Next a large rusty hook was produced and a bundle of washers served as sinkers. To this odd assortment of tackle he added a big chunk of clam meat with all the flair of a gourmet chef. I watched, fascinated, as the strange lure splashed overboard. The ritual continued with big handfuls of sacrificial ground bait scattered on the water. The stuff was made from oatmeal and bits of chopped-up bar clams. "Pogey, poooooooooooogee!" yelled our George, the high priest of the mackerel kingdom.

The chant echoed across the ruffled water. "Poooogee." The cry rang out like a summons in the same manner a farmer would call hens or hogs. In a flash he had a big mackerel dancing green and blue on the end of the rusty hook. A flip and a flick of his wrist to land it in the bottom of the boat, and so started the slaughter.

I fumbled excitedly with my lightweight nylon rod and costly reel, scattering the shiny new jigs all over the wet floorboards. All the hootchy-kootchies and toy squid things went flying, and one of them hooked my pants. Another speared my thumb. "George," I announced quite confidently, "these are guaranteed to catch the big ones." My "correct weight" line tangled in a mighty knot, the top section of the rod went over the side, and once again the ancient mariner flipped another mackerel into the bottom of the boat with a smooth action of jerk, flip, release, and cast while I just flailed the surface of the water. George and the fish laughed at my audacity to think I'd actually catch one of them. Mind you, I did catch my fishing companion once or twice and so learned some colorful additions to the language of Maritime Canada.

This mackerel massacre went on for some time until more than a dozen of them were swimming around the bottom of the boat. "Wait a minute!" I cried. "They're bloody well swimming in here, George. We're filling up with water." The waves at the mouth of the river were growing whitecaps and of course there were no life vests aboard the *Luxury Lady*. Below us fifty feet of dark water waited. I pulled the lid off my new tackle box, and using it like a scoop, started bailing like mad.

Montague River water was bubbling into the Vatcher yacht quite rapidly. Soon the juicy mackerel would be returning to their natural habitat. No doubt George and I would be joining them! He flipped one more fat fish into his new half-floating fishtank. Then as casual as you like he took up the oars, just as the first mackerel jumped to freedom and safety. I could almost hear it calling to its mates, "Come on, boys, jump, before you all drown!" The others probably answered back, "Why, we're already safe in the water!" A couple more rolled up and over the side. Now my shipmate leaned to the oars with a good deal of cursing as the water reached the seat of his trousers.

Once more I scraped through yet another soggy nightmare in my ocean quest. I waded ashore with the water up to my chest. George hurled a couple of the remaining mackerel onto the beach so that our fishing expedition would not be a total loss. "Well, dear," said George, "you and the missus will have a lovely feed for yer dinner. Yer a great little fisherman but you can play that banjo better!" He broke into a great fit of laughter at his own joke. Dripping and cold, I contemplated bodily harm on this long-lost "odd" man. He pulled a half bottle of rum from his coat pocket. "Here ya go, darlin'! Take a slap o' that stuff. That'll straighten yer rudder." He broke into another fit of wild, wheezing roars, taking a few swallows to "get the old motor goin'."

When old Eli discovered his dangerous son had the rum, he came down the beach to join the merriment. The pack of mangy dogs were leaping about, glad to see their master had survived another day on the sea. Two or three of them attacked each other when they discovered the freshly landed mackerel. These were fish-eating dogs.

I hurried away home leaving my dinner, the dogs, and the two old plunderers to their nightly rampage with Captain Morgan. It was not the first time that a pile of salty wet clothes would lie on my bathroom floor as I hurriedly and hypothermically drew a scalding bath. With the words of another old "go-to-sea-no-more" song chattering through my sodden thoughts, I lay back and smiled as I sank into more comforting and forgiving waters.

Ghosts and Phantom ships

O ur ancient mariner, George Vatcher, got a lot of pleasure from giving people presents and we were never sure where he acquired these gifts, although I am confident that he came by them honestly. One misty day I looked across the field and spotted a strange apparition rolling up the long driveway. It was George, dressed as usual in that long navy greatcoat and riding a child's bike obtained from my musical friend Dennis Ryan, a native of Tipperary who lived a mile away on the other side of our extraordinary neighbor.

George was making his long legs pedal that small bicycle, his big knees flying up to his chin. Streaming out above his head was a long yellow banner. When he arrived, puffing and blowing, I saw that the streamer was actually a long evening gown. It had a full-length cape down the back and a strapless top and looked to me like a vintage 1957 creation. Hat in hand he announced in a grand sort of way, "I brought a gift for the little lady, dear. I want her to wear it for her birthday." The dress was remarkably new looking and smelled of mothballs and a vague overtone of Eau de Vatcher perfume. I smiled and called Catherine to come down to the kitchen and get her gift.

He took off his captain's cap when she arrived and gave her a big smelly hug. "Come on now, dear," I said to her with devilish glee. "Go and try on that dress for George. It's simply you, dahling." Well, like the trouper that she is, up she went and returned shortly, swishing down the stairs like Scarlett O'Hara and looking like a million dollars in the George Vatcher creation. "Wow!" I cried. "Hold that pose!"

She minced and vamped down the stairs, ending the performance with a throaty, "Come up and see me sometime."

I looked at George and to my surprise he was brushing a tear away from his eye, but a drink of rum straightened him up, and he started to sing his favorite song, "A Mother's Love's a Blessing." I found out later that the dress belonged to the only woman who had ever been in George's life—his mother. He told me that he still owed money for her funeral and for his own headstone. I went down and saw that grave marker one day. Not only was his mother's name inscribed but so were the two surviving Vatcher men, Eli and George himself. The year of their birth was marked and beside the year of death was a blank. "Why did you put your name on that stone, George?" I asked him one day.

"Well, dear, when I'm gone, who's gonna do it for me?"

George with a fine pair of clam-digging feet

George was full of superstitions and he loved to tell you about the haunted houses on the Island. He even claimed that the old Clarke house where we lived had a ghost. "I seen it, dear," he whispered with great conviction. The house sat on old sandstone foundations that used to support a grander home owned by a governor of the Island. His name was Wightman and locals still called our property Wightman's Point. "She was a Negro maid," whispered George, "murdered here a hundred years ago." We laughed, but on dark winter nights when the whole place would groan and creak in a storm, the story would come back and creep eerily round my thoughts.

George and Eli lived in a tumbledown shack with another bigger shack built over top of it. Some of the local carpenters had got together, with a little government help, and erected a new roof and walls. The old building was left trapped inside with the idea that it would give the Vatchers a place to live while the new home was constructed. Unfortunately they never moved out of the old home, and the new outer building became a place for dogs and ducks and stressed-out hens. So in their fortlike setting they survived on Eli's war pension and on welfare, or, as George called it, "the pokey." He did odd jobs on people's boats and earned a few dollars to buy tobacco and gin.

The Vatchers had a telephone, and I'm not sure how they managed that but I heard it was arranged by the local doctor, since George was the only caregiver for old Eli, who was over ninety. George was a pest with that telephone for he would call me at odd hours to ask for something, or simply to sing me my next hit song, which he had just written. Catherine was remarkably kind and polite to him and I tried my best to follow her example.

There was a night, however, when my patience was sorely

tested by our colorful neighbor. Catherine and I had just burrowed down into the warmth of five or six blankets. A gale was raging and hammering the boards on that lonely exposed farmhouse on St. Andrew's Point. Only a few scrub spruce survived on the red clay cliffs and offered no windbreak against the Atlantic winds that pounded like a massive fist against the windows and ancient, high-peaked roof.

You could hear the whole house protest. Lying in bed during a storm felt like being at sea. The waves would roar close by and the roof had a frightening way of breathing with the wind. The chandelier would catch the rhythm of the rafters, and we would both stare in disbelief as it started its swinging motion. I sometimes felt that we had become a wooden ship blown out to sea and were creaking along on the stormy wave.

On that night the phone lines were somehow still up and working for a noisy ring made us both jump. I looked at the clock beside the bed and it was nearly midnight. Trying to stay under the covers I swiped out to grab the phone and in doing so knocked the clock, a vase, the phone, and myself onto the cold floor. I sat in the spilled water from the vase and the cheery voice of George yelled at me, "Did ye see the light, dear?"

I managed to get the phone to my ear and said rather angrily, "What? What bloody light, George?"

"Well, dear," he continued rather mysteriously, "you and the missus get down there to the shore and take a look!" Then to my utter frustration he hung up.

I told Catherine there must be some trouble on the water and I was going to take a look. "Are you nuts? In this weather? Yes!" she said, answering her own question. She volunteered to join the mission to the stormy beach at the bottom of our farmlands. "I couldn't sleep anyway," she said with a laugh.

Covered in blankets and leaning into the gale, we squelched through the muddy pathway to the edge of the roaring ocean.

Churning breakers were pounding our now mutilated beach. We stood close to the shore, our faces stinging from the blowing sand and drenched by spray and rain. "What are we supposed to be looking for?" she asked. "What did George say?"

"All he said was to go down and check for a light," I muttered.

We searched the darkness for some ship in distress or anything else that seemed odd. Nothing. Only the distant stab of light from the Panmure Island beacon. "I think I will throttle our George Vatcher!" I yelled. Catherine started laughing and I did a mad freezing dance in my red long johns. We ran home together soaked to the skin, lit a fire, and poured ourselves a hot buttered rum.

It was now about one-thirty in the morning and I thought I would pay old George back so I phoned him and let it ring a dozen times. Finally he came on the line with a wild yell. "HALOOOOO THERE!" He complained that I had awakened him from a dream about hundreds of gin bottles floating up on the shore and no one but him and his daddy to gather in the crop.

"George, what in hell was I supposed to see down at the beach?"

"The ship," he replied, and hung up.

I met him the next day in the liquor store and discovered that his ship was a phantom. "Me and Daddy have seen her many times, dear," he related seriously. "She's on fire and there's a woman on the deck holding a wee child. The flames light up the sky and it passes right there in front of your house, from Panmure Island to Georgetown headland. We saw it last night and that's why I phoned you, dear. I wanted you to take a photo of her for me. They'll pay me a lot of money on the TV for that photo!"

Catherine looked at me and smiled. I took a couple of beer out of the six-pack I had just purchased and dropped them into his greatcoat pocket. "George," I said, "give us a call the next time you see that ship, OK. I want to see that for myself."

He was quite amazed that we had not seen his phantom ship. "It's supposed to be a sign of bad luck you know," he added mysteriously.

I spoke to my friend and local newspaper editor Jim McNeill, and he told me that the phantom ship story has persisted for a century around that part of the Island. Many people had reported seeing a burning ship out there on the water. He told me of a possible origin of the story that dated back to the time when Prince Edward Island was controlled by the French and was called Île Ste. Jean.

A French emigrant ship coming into Georgetown, which lay across the bay from our home, caught fire in the galley just as she was about to anchor. The fire spread rapidly and crackled out of control through the ship. Everyone got off except a woman and her baby. She was the wife of the new governor, and as she cried for help, her husband went mad with grief on the shore, forced to watch helplessly as the ship went down in flames. I've often wondered if it's only souls like George, who are closer to nature and mystical things than those of us who depend on modern electronic entertainment, that are able to experience phantom lights and ships from the dark regions.

The last time I saw George Vatcher he looked much older than his forty-eight years. His father, Eli, had been admitted to the old people's home. I was heading out to the airport, where I would fly out to meet the Irish Rovers in Vancouver. Having a bit of time I stopped my car when I saw George shoveling the first October snow from his pathway. "How're ya, George?" I yelled.

"Oh, I'm a bit lonely, dear, since they took Daddy to the

Manor." I asked him if he would let me videotape a greeting from him to my father who was now back home with my mother, in a little house on Sea Island near Vancouver. My Da had always got along well with him, and I knew he'd be pleased to see George on video.

He was shy in front of the camera, but he soon warmed up when I gave him ten dollars to buy a "pint." He sent best wishes to "Bobbie," as he called him, as well as a few humorous little anecdotes and a tuneless song. I turned off the camera and packed it back into my satchel. Just before I pulled away he said to me in a worried voice, "I seen that ghost ship two nights ago, and dear," he continued, "you might not believe this but there was someone standing on the burning deck." At this point he leaned over and whispered in my ear. "Do you know who that person was? It was myself, dear!"

I looked at this strangest of men and got a chilly feeling that I would never see him again. I was right. Two weeks after I left on my next tour, poor George was lost somewhere on the sea, hopefully hunting for that thousand-pound black-fin tuna.

For nearly six years we had George Vatcher as our neighbor and when I look back on it now, I realize I gained a wealth of stories and laughter from all of his mad antics. I have related his tales around the world. His yarns of phantom ships and dreadful sea monsters (and he had no doubt about their existence) have become a part of our family folk legacy. I heard my little eight-year-old daughter Clare telling her girlfriends a George Vatcher tale just the other day. So old George, whatever messy part of sailor's heaven you are cruising, your tales are not forgotten. Long may they spin!

Last year when I visited the Island, I stopped at the Vatchers' grave. There was still a blank space beside the year of his passing and I thought, "Just right too, that's the way it should be. Life is short enough. No need to tell the world when the voyage ended." I hope that if anyone chances upon the Vatcher grave marker in Lower Montague, they will wonder if old George is still around. He probably is anyway, living on some island out there beyond Boughten. Where whole cargoes of rum and gin and tobacco get washed up every week. Where mackerel leap up out of the waves and jump into his dirty old frying pan. Where he and his mother and old Eli live forever, to remind us that there's more to life than the mad quest for perfection and success.

ELEVENTH VERSE

Sinn fein means... ourselves alone

Diary entry from the days of Windflower Downs

In the woods near my lighted house, by a peaceful clearing overgrown with bay bushes and mossy ferns, four walls stand silently crumbling. The boards break away at the touch and a rabbit bolts for cover from beneath the rusty remains of a New Brunswick stove. The walls that were built from the local fir and spruce against the Island winters are little use now after fifty years of neglect and bound to return to their forest floor.

Here and there around this coast I come across these deserted homes, and a wave will wash across my thinking—a kind of lingering sadness like a hunger pain—a need to know the story of who the people were who built these houses and walked these forest paths so long ago. If only some magic would allow me to stand beyond the tumbled door and have all the scenes that played within, since the house began, come back to me in color and sound. The homespun faces, the songs and smell of new bread and lye soap. To see the children who found their way to an eight-

hour day in Toronto or Halifax, or the ones that the
sea took, boats and traps and all.

I come sometimes to walk within those empty
walls in the forest clearing near my place, to remind
myself how important every moment is to me on this
Island. Before my walls crumble I must fill them with
love and light and laughter, with music and children—
and a bottomless bucket of paint.

—August 1979

By 1980, Catherine and I had grown close to the Island
seaside farm. It had been a good year and the Irish Rovers had
a surprising hit song called "Wasn't That a Party." But with the
party in full swing around the world, it meant I would be away
even more than ever. The touring year usually commenced in
early March so I asked Catherine in mid-February to take a
special trip back to Kona with me, where we had met four
years earlier. In that same sunny village where I first fell in love
with her I asked if she would consider marrying me. When she
said she would, I felt an incredible surge of life float down
those lava hillsides from the old Mauna Kea volcano,
engulfing me in that warm coast full of joy. Matthew Anderson
and the missionary's child were reunited once more and ready
for another circle of seasons.

We recruited the services of a Kahuna—a Hawaiian priest—
and in a simple ceremony up on the hillside near "Captain
Cook" at Kealakekua Bay, we were married. The cooing of
mourning doves, the chorus of singing birds, and the rhythm
of Hawaiian music was better to us than any orchestrated
wedding in the finest church in the world. I will remember that
special time all my life. Catherine in her missionary's dress
looked for all the world like the girl in that lucid dream of five
years earlier.

It was bitter cold when we returned to our other Island after our short stay in Hawaii. The flights to Charlottetown had been cancelled and so we sailed on the ferry. It was an eerie and bleak experience after lush and colorful Hawaii. The searchlight beacon from the ship played its light out on the frozen ocean, and the boat crunched along with a grinding noise as it cracked great chunks of ice to bring us back home. It was then that we first started talking about moving back to the West Coast and to a milder climate. "It will be difficult to raise kids out here in the winter," she said with the hint of a promise. "What will I do when you're gone and I'm at the end of an unpaved road with a new baby?"

She kept that promise and our first wee boy was born in the old hospital in Charlottetown. Below the hospital room window, that first morning, the small fleet of boats in the harbor waved their pennants in the breeze in an Island welcome. I had waited for this event for years and for the first few months I couldn't leave my new son alone. I played the tin whistle to him, took him out on my rowboat (when Catherine was too tired to notice), and I danced him round the floor singing old sea chanteys. It's true that the first child usually receives an overdose of stimulation, and there never was a shortage of babysitters since the daughters of the Murphy clan adored the little dark-eyed soul. Now we were part of the Island, no longer "from away" since one of our family was a native-born son of Prince Edward Island.

We made quite a few changes to the old farmhouse that first year of James's growing, and there was very little time for outdoor recreation. But as time went on I grew tired of just puddling around in a rowboat and I felt that the only thing missing in my life was a real ocean-going boat. Small islands on that blue horizon were calling out to me. Once in a while I sailed out past them as a passenger in some lobster boat and

I wanted to explore their deserted beaches. There was history in these waters that I needed to explore, and I couldn't do it without a sturdy boat to convey me away from the land.

One morning at breakfast Catherine casually mentioned, "What's this I hear about you buying a boat?" She had heard from Karen Murphy that I had put an offer on a six-ton lobster boat. I hadn't told her about it because it was just one of those hypnotic impulse boat cravings that strike me without warning. I had been out with Gerard Murphy and he had shown me a fine-looking Cape Islander, the much-respected wooden boat of the inshore Canadian Maritime fisheries. It was anchored down at a quiet little bay called French Creek. The deal was struck quickly and for the humble sum of a thousand dollars she was mine.

The *Norma Jean* was a bare wooden hull with just a small wheelhouse. She measured forty feet overall and below decks a powerful 292 Chev engine kicked off with a roar midships, while a smoky tailpipe polluted the air on the river. Somehow, she seemed right for this time in my life. It seems, when I look back on it, that I was trying hard to be a real Islander. I didn't

The freshly painted, rebuilt Shin Jane

want to appear like a big city yachtsman with a plastic boat so I drove an old beat-up pickup truck and now, to complete the picture, I had a twenty-year-old wooden boat—a real Island boat.

I always had great disdain for "smoke pots," but now I was ready to take one under my command. I had already planned to rename her *Shin Fane*, which is phonetic Irish for "sinn fein" or ourselves alone. Sailing was always a personal thing to me, and I suppose I always dreamed of solo adventures on the sea. I reasoned *Shin Fane* was an appropriate name. Sailors say it is unlucky to change the name of a boat, but I scoffed at those old superstitions. I put a lot of time into the *Shin Fane* during the short summers with tons of new paint and extensive interior work. Before long she was transformed from a rough old workhorse to quite a comfortable cruiser. A brand-new fuel tank was installed, the engine was tuned up, there were lots of life jackets aboard, and even the dingy was shipshape. My wife suggested one day that perhaps I should install a ship-to-home phone line since I spent so much time just sitting out there at anchor, scrubbing, painting, and scraping, in the endless ritual of the wooden boat worshipper.

The view from the skylight of the seaside farmhouse will always be one of my favorite Island memories: I could gaze across the lush verdant fields, over the red sandstone beach to the sparkling ocean and admire my white wooden boat at anchor. Sometimes, Catherine and I would sit on the doorstep facing the sea, drinking our morning tea, and I would wax poetic about the fine sturdy lines and perfect design of the Cape Islander, although my beloved companion did not share my adoration for the old wooden boat.

She had heard, by this time, all about my "mishaps" at sea and was learning to keep safely away from me when I had the urge to set sail. "I'm glad you like it," she'd say with a smile.

"But it's so far out from the shore. Why don't you park it closer to the beach, or take it to the wharf in town?" I liked having the boat near the house so I put up with a long hike out across the shallows. At low tide the first couple of hundred yards were only two feet deep and it was a nuisance having the *Shin Fane* anchored so far from the shore.

I had dropped a four-cylinder engine block into about eight feet of water and attached the *Shin Fane* to it with a length of yellow nylon rope. The fishermen told me I really needed a big truck engine block to anchor a boat of that weight, but this old Morris Minor engine had been lying in the shed and it seemed heavy enough to me.

Now and then I climbed aboard the *Shin Fane* with a stiff wind singing and the dingy would get away from me leaving me stranded aboard; that was irritation enough. It was worse when the six-and-a-half-ton fishing boat broke loose and headed out to sea. One particular break for freedom sticks clearly in my mind and has earned its place near the top of my list of dangerous ocean stunts.

A storm had been brewing all morning and I was going around the outside of the house to batten down the hatches when some premonition made me stop in mid-stride and I stared wildly out to sea. She was gone! Instead of bobbing at her anchor, my proud and spunky Cape Islander appeared as a tiny dot rolling and bucking toward the Cape Breton horizon. I raced into the water up to my knees, waving my arms like windmills in an attempt to get her to return. This Chaplinesque routine didn't seem to have much effect, so I began running up and down the beach in a mad frenzy, feeling like one of the nonbelievers standing in the rain as Noah's ark sailed away.

The sky was turning leaden and dirty. Churning green waves and whitecaps were pounding at the shore when I leaped into

my old Cherokee Chief and tore down the clay road toward the
fishing shacks at Pooles Wharf. Most of the lobster boats had
returned for the day, and a few fishermen were playing cards in
the warehouse where they stored their traps for the winter. I
burst in, wild-eyed, with a plea for help. "I'll give any one of
you a forty-ouncer of Captain Morgan if you'll take me out
after my boat." Not one of them turned from his serious
poker playing. I suppose I was still a landlubber in their eyes.
They made their living out there in the deep and boats were
merely the tools of their trade. No sea fever burned in these
lobstermen's souls and they looked forward to the end of the
season when they could pull the boats ashore for another
year. I do believe they were quite intolerant of haphazard and
amateurish seamanship.

It hadn't taken me long to build a reputation with the
seafaring folk along the river, and a couple of them had
already towed me back home a few times when the infernal
engine trouble struck. I had pretty much worn out my welcome
in the rescue department, but Billy McKinnon was tempted by
the Captain Morgan. He took the bottle and stuck it in his
oilskin coat. Even though he was already a few sheets to the
wind, he took another long draw out of the rum as we boarded
the dingy to row out to his big yellow V-hull, *The Naughty
Nancy*, which was anchored in the middle of the river.

The wind blew us back and forward, and it took fifteen
minutes of hard rowing before we could finally scramble out of
the punt and into the pitch and roll of the big scallop dragger.
Billy cranked up the powerful engine and away we roared into
the wild ocean, dipping nose under with mighty splashes and
flying salt spray. The waves were running about fifteen feet, as
high as the cabin roof, and every so often one larger than the
rest crashed over our bow in a booming surge. A pod of
porpoises raced us joyfully as we headed further away from

shore accompanied by Billy singing some delicate verses of "The North Atlantic Squadron." I was scanning the stormy, heaving horizon for my runaway *Shin Fane* as we plowed east past Boughten Island. Five miles offshore I spotted her rocking sideways in the choppy rollers.

As we drew near I could see the yellow nylon anchor line stretched tight over the side. Obviously the four-cylinder engine block anchor was still attached and I decided the fishermen had been right about the truck engine block. At high tide, *Shin Fane* had simply picked up the small block and taken off on her joyful escape.

When *The Naughty Nancy* rolled alongside my carefree vessel, Billy handed me a rusty fish knife. "You'll have to jump aboard and cut that block free. Then if she won't start, I'll throw you a tow rope." I looked at Billy in disbelief and back at the pitching deck of the *Shin Fane.*

"What!" I yelled. "Are you crazy?" He answered with a fiendish laugh, and I knew that he was indeed.

I should have wondered about my own sanity at that point for I grabbed the knife in my teeth and, feeling like Errol Flynn in a pirate picture, I leaped out onto the drunken foredeck and landed with a crash. I was immediately flattened onto the deck and there I lay, spread-eagled, winded, in fear for my life, and leaving teeth marks on the handle of the knife. I closed my eyes for a moment and lay there in mortal terror of being pitched into the sea.

Once again I was caught in a dangerous situation, fully clothed, wearing wide-mouth gumboots and no life vest. I knew that I would sink like a stone out there in no time at all. In desperation I started to hack and saw away at the new nylon hawser line while grimly hanging on with one hand to a small wooden cleat. Finally the Morris Minor engine block broke free and hurtled to the ocean bottom.

I lay for a moment almost calm in the teeth of this potentially deadly experience. The roll of the boat was frightful, and I was sure that at any moment I would be flung into the ominous deep. Gritting my teeth I started to crawl my way aft to the wheelhouse inch by inch. It seemed like an eternity as one minute I would be level with the surface of the water, then another roll and I'd be six feet above the foam. Everything below in the cabin was smashing about and I bit my lip till it bled and crawled on. Finally I made it into the wheelhouse to try to get her under way. When I turned the key there were a few splutters, and a great belch of smoke billowed up out of the stack. Then with a great rush of relief, I heard the engine roar into life.

I waved triumphantly over to Billy in *The Naughty Nancy*. He waved back and took another gulp of the Captain Morgan rum. Then for some unknown reason he wheeled around and took off in a great wake of foam. I guess he was anxious to get home to his naughty Nancy—whoever she was. I knew then that I had made a big mistake by giving him the rum before the job was complete. I tried yelling for him to come back and follow me to make sure everything was all right but he was long out of earshot.

"Oh, holy mackerel!" I screamed, or perhaps something just a little more profound. "Wait a minute to see if she keeps goin'." I had no sooner uttered the words than the engine stopped and once more I was adrift five miles from shore with a fading battery and the sky showing the first signs of evening.

I cursed *The Naughty Nancy* and called her rum-sotted skipper every wild and abusive name I could think up. I cursed the *Shin Fane* and her fickle engine. I yelled horrible oaths at the elements and at the entire Island race. The seas were tumbling me in a rolling motion and all I could do was hang on and try not to get flung about.

After half an hour, the wind died down as it always seems
to do on the Island toward late afternoon. I was grateful to
have Shin Fane stabilized once again. But now I had to worry
about getting back to shore. The lighter winds were urging me
along and I was relieved to discover they were heading me in a
landward direction toward the distant Souris shoreline. I was
too angry to be seasick or even a bit nervous and I decided to
give up trying to start the engine. Instead I used the remaining
battery power to call the Coast Guard.

Just the week before, on Catherine's urging, I had installed
a CB radio. Now it was my lifeline to some invisible rescuers. I
spoke to quite a few voices who passed on the word to the
Coast Guard, and I could have kissed the radio when a voice
sounding like Lorne Green from Bonanza said, "This is the
Souris Coast Guard, come in." I jumped into action, twiddling
every knob and pushing every button in my anxiety to be
heard. I finally got them to hear me on channel 16 and
received confirmation that they were on their way.

I opened up a good old Schooner beer and sat back in my
rickety captain's chair. The wind had died away to a breeze
and I said a quiet, thankful prayer that it would stay that way.
I lit my antique ship's lantern—a relic of a schooner that
foundered on the Irish coast. I had screwed it to the bulkhead
the day before and filled it up with kerosene. Now it glowed in
the gathering dusk and I rocked along as the Shin Fane drifted
in the breeze toward the lights on shore. I threw out a fishing
line and waited to catch a Coast Guard vessel.

Good old Marconi. What would helpless ocean waifs do
without you? Good old Coast Guard as well, you are an
important part of us poor sailors' lives. I wonder, do they sell
shares in the Coast Guard—I'd like to have a few! The last
light of the day was disappearing over an orange-colored
ocean when I spotted their powerful boat coming toward me

in a grand shower of spray. They came aboard to check me out and soon had me under tow at a right good clip heading toward my friendly shore and the lights of Lower Montague.

We steered the *Shin Fane* down to the wharf until such time as I could drop a more substantial anchor and replace the engine. I invited the boys from the Coast Guard back home with me for tea and a feed of "moonlight" lobster. (On rare nights I would row out and visit an out-of-season lobster trap. I got to recognize the telltale vinegar bottle floats that marked the illegal trap. I would remove a fat juicy lobster and leave a bottle of beer in its place for the unknown poacher.)

Catherine was quite surprised when she arrived home from a day in Charlottetown to find the kitchen filled with uniformed men. "Don't tell me, boys," she laughed. "I do not want to know, but thank you all very much for whatever you had to do to save this man."

Thank you, lads, wherever you are today. *Shin Fane*'s name would be on your rescue slates one more time before too long.

TWELFTH VERSE

Last hurrahs and Pacific horizons

*M*y music life was forcing me to be away more often than ever, and I felt glum and lonely each time I kissed Catherine and my little boy good-bye. Years later Catherine told me they used to watch the red taillights of my departing taxi until it disappeared down the clay road. Then a great depression would set in for her as she prepared for lonely housebound weeks, especially in the dead of winter when she would be unable to get out for walks in that fierce climate. One day my little son saw my open suitcase lying on the floor as I was packing to leave. I found him lying inside the suitcase, determined to travel with me, away from the winter to meet his cousins and grandparents out West. It broke my heart, and I believe it was on that day we finally made the decision to move so that Catherine could be near her family.

It was difficult and emotional for us to put the house on the market. We were told by the realtors that it would take a long time to sell such a unique and remote home. But a buyer came along sooner than any of us expected and suddenly we both felt quite lost. We had spent many happy days round those Windflower Downs, and a new baby boy had taken his first steps across the old maple floors. We were now a part of the Island, but the die was cast and we were heading west at the end of the summer.

Six years earlier, when I first arrived on that warm summer day, I knew part of my destiny lay in and around those red sandstone shores, and I have been very grateful ever since. The days I spent on that island were the most fulfilling ones of my life. Now we were packing all our pack rat treasures and the final good-byes, we knew, would be painful.

We noticed the Island was changing, and we were both glad we had found it when we did. We used to have the lands and woods all to ourselves. Now the developers had discovered our hideaway and had turned sections of the old seaside farm fields into cottage lots. Old characters were disappearing and before long a fixed-link bridge would make the Island a part of mainland Nova Scotia.

I was determined to make this last summer a memorable one and as it turned out some of the memories I could well have done without. The last voyage for me aboard the *Shin*

Shin Jane heading out to the open sea

Fane started out on a peaceful early fall day. My wife and our little baby boy were joined by the Ellis family and their four children. "Big John" with his long red ponytail looked for all the world like one of the imaginary Viking raiders of my Irish childhood. As we ferried the kids out to the *Shin Fane* aboard the little rowboat, my two-year-old insisted on sitting on my knee and trying the oars. He loved boats and the ocean and I felt content in the full cycle of life.

We had packed boxes of food and a tin of gas, an extra battery and replacement fan belts, cooler, lots of life jackets, flares and extra rope, water and everything else needed for a picnic on the deserted beaches of Boughten Island. I had tested the CB radio—just in case. Then I said a silent prayer to Neptune that I would not be needing any of these emergency provisions.

Shin Fane sounded healthy enough with a freshly tuned engine, a reconditioned fuel pump, and a new gas tank. She had a good strong dingy in tow, complete with a nine-horsepower motor. Just your simple sailor's life on the ocean wave. What a day! A five-mile sail across a calm ocean under a brilliant blue sky. I called out to the company, "It doesn't get much better than this, my friends."

All the kids were singing, "Sailing, sailing, over the bounding main" and "Jack was every inch a sailor." I smiled and sang along and performed an impromptu sailor's hornpipe, but my ears were always listening to the sound of the engine. There had been so much trouble with the beast that I knew the signs of impending disaster. Today, there simply could not be any problems.

It's always a worry when you take small children offshore. I have friends who have cruised the world with their babies. "Didn't bother them in the least!" they say, but I'm sure I would be a nervous wreck. Now a little stab of worry nagged, like the beginning of a toothache, as I noticed a slight change of rhythm in the stroke of the engine.

I kept my eye on the last red clay bank of Prince Edward Island headland and the Panmure lighthouse. For some reason *Shin Fane* always gave me trouble about a mile offshore. That 292 Chev engine seemed to run smoothly just long enough to get me into deep water. Then some gremlin would crawl into the machinery.

No one else noticed the change in the engine as a few little beats started missing. I held my breath and cruised on by the Panmure light with a sigh of hope and relief. A flurry of wind ruffled my pennant, and now I could see the shining beaches of Boughten. "Wait till you get ashore," I told my first-time passengers. "You'll love it! There are old houses on Boughten that have been deserted since the twenties and they're haunted." The kids gasped in mock fear and everyone was excited. The mood was cheery until about half a mile off the beach.

It happened instantly; one moment we were singing along under full power, the next silence. Everyone looked at me, and I lightheartedly produced a foolish laugh. "Ha! Ha! Noooo problem." Catherine groaned and commenced to dress all the children in life vests.

"Okay kids, come on, I think we're going ashore in the dingy." She was right. Half an hour later we drifted close enough to the beach of little Boughten Island to safely disembark, and thank God the sea was calm enough to get all the kids into the dingy with only five feet of water under our hull. I threw out the anchor and my friend John, as calm as ever, ferried everyone ashore to the beach.

I kicked the cover off the engine and when I was sure I was alone, and even though I had been practicing my yoga meditation faithfully for more than a year, I went through yet one more berserk session of insults to every timber, plank, bilge sludge, and bolt on that damn engine. I hammered the valve cover with a wrench and threw cans against the inside of the hull. "Why in the name of all that's holy am I so cursed in boats?" I yelled at the heathen gods of the deep. "What did I ever do to you down there or up there? Why me!" Then the primal scream. "I'll never go near another boat in my entire life!" A distant summer thunder echoed and somewhere I heard the Sovereign of the Seas snicker with a gargling, hollow rumble.

Then, that yoga calmness came over me, as well as another calmness learned through years of experience on troubled seas. My true sailor's instinct kicked in and I lay down on the deck, picked up an old canvas life jacket and pounded it to within a fiber of its being. John came back and I told him in a wild, despairing voice that once more *Shin Fane* was dead in the water. Now John, as I've said, is a very easygoing kind of man, not easily flustered, and would probably make a fine offshore sailor. He suggested, quietly, that we take the dingy back to the shore and talk to our wives.

The children were splashing in the warm shallow water, and Eva and Catherine were gathering armfuls of driftwood to prepare an overnight fire to keep us warm on that deserted Atlantic island. "Ach, don't worry," I tried to assure them. "I'll have us under way long before evening." My wife paused for a moment, then without a word the two women continued their survival mission. I think I heard one of them mutter, "Right! Sure thing, Captain!" as they piled up their night's firewood.

John wondered if the two of us should take the dingy across from the far east end of Boughten Island, which was a much shorter run to the mainland than coming from St. Andrew's Point. I agreed that we could probably make it since the weather was so calm, but Catherine said to me quite emphatically that I shouldn't even think of such a plan. "It's only half a mile or so," I told her. "That's an easy little jaunt for the nine-horsepower Johnson." The children were having a great time, and the sun was warm as we motored away from the beach. Catherine yelled, "Good luck and be careful," and Eva retorted with some words in her native Polish.

"What does that mean, my dear?" asked John grinning.

"I hope you paid up your insurance policy," she answered with a laugh.

"We'll be back in about an hour," I shouted as we pushed off, trying to sound as if John and I were just taking a pleasant little sail.

They watched our small boat until we disappeared behind a cliff, then the families settled down to a lovely afternoon's picnic. The *Shin Fane* was just nodding out there with a guilty tugging of her anchor. "Sail! Sail! That would be the answer here, John," I raved. "I should have stayed with a real boat, instead of a smoky, smelly gas-guzzling old whore of a fishing boat. How stupid can I be! Right now we could be skimming in the summer breeze round the Island with good old nature as our power source. I was never meant to own a fishing boat without a sail. I-am-a-SAILOR! John, I should be under sail."

John was about to soothe me with some of his homespun wisdom when the engine on the dingy stopped abruptly. I stared at him in disbelief. He tried to restart it with a few pulls of the rope, but it was unresponsive. I tried a few times as well, each pull becoming more wild and frustrated. "I hate engines that have rope pulls! I hate chain saws and lawn mowers! I detest old outboards and I curse the man who ever invented them!" John was laughing at my tirade and I gave another herculean pull on the starter rope only to have it break loose, sending me overboard with a wild yell and a splash. John hauled me aboard, almost overturning the dingy.

I sat there in a silent, soaking rage as John took up the oars and headed back to the picnic. "First I want you to take me to the *Shin Fane*," I said.

"Why?" asked John.

"I want to burn her with me aboard. I've always wanted a Viking funeral." John got a good laugh out of that remark as well. He set to with the oars and we rowed back the way we had come until he landed me against the side of the stranded *Shin Fane*. "I'm going to change and then I'm going to start calling my old friends at the Coast Guard." John rowed ashore and the women and children gave him a grand round of applause. He stood up in the boat, gave a sweeping bow, and to complete the comedy performed a mighty belly flop right into the water. I could hear their merriment as I tuned into the Coast Guard channel.

"Hello, come in, this is the *Shin Fane*. Can you read me? Over." The first response I received on the radio came from a trucker with a southern accent. He was picking up my signal somewhere on the Boston turnpike.

Finally, after hearing from a few dozen well-wishers in a variety of locations, a welcoming voice announced: "This is Souris Coast Guard, come in?"

"This is the *Shin Fane*," I repeated. "Come in."

The Coast Guard responded with, "Repeat, did you say champagne?"

"No, no! Come back," I said. "*Shin Fane*." They kept repeating "Champagne, Champagne," so I yelled, "OK! OK! Champagne."

Back on the shore, my ever tolerant wife could hear me yelling from the boat. "Oh my God," she exclaimed, "he's finally flipped. He's asking for champagne."

We had a two-hour wait for our rescue party, so I thought I would tinker with the eternal-infernal, cursed engine monster. It started with a roar a couple of times, but just as quickly it would cut out. Then I discovered that by taking a drop or two of gasoline and pouring it directly into the carburetor, I could get the engine to kick over for a minute or so. "Well," I thought, "if I can do this, I just might be able to make it back home without the Coast Guard."

Then with a kerpluffe! and a whoosh! the gas ignited in the carburetor. I dropped the pop can full of fuel that I had been using to spark the engine and the can promptly went up in flames. I jumped away and ran up on deck, desperately rummaging around looking for the fire extinguisher. I had brought everything I could think of but the fire extinguisher was still in its original box at home in my shed. Lovely, bloody lovely! A can of oil had spilled in the bilge under the engine and the fire began to spread down there as well. I had no intention of going down with the ship, and since we were in just six feet of water, I did what I had done in the dingy only an hour before, except this time it was voluntary. I tumbled over the side and struck out for shore. John saw the smoke and was already on his way to pick me up.

In horrible fascination we stood on the beach and watched the fire grow until ugly orange flames were leaping out of the wheelhouse windows. My mind raced to my other catastrophes while messing about in boats. If there is such a thing as karma and reincarnation, I must have been up to no good in my last sailing life. I have heard it said, by people who firmly believe, that we carry the same traits from life to life, until we finally reach an understanding of what is wrong with our attitude and mend our ways. "I'm trying, I'm trying," I thought. "Is there anyone up there with a bit of nautical advice?"

The *Shin Fane* was burning. Black smoke was rising skywards, and woeful sounds of whining and popping were part of her death rattle. I do believe the old girl was crying. I lay on the beach holding my head, staring in disbelief at the cremation of another dream and numb with shock. I wanted to do something but I was at a loss and George Vatcher's story of the phantom ship came to mind. The kids were very upset so the women took them for a walk over the sand dunes to the old houses, leaving John and I alone with the horror.

I watched the black smoke rising above the tall spruce trees. It was one of the most eerie feelings I've ever had. Fire and water are my birth signs, but this was not easy to accept. The fire burned through the hull first at the waterline and salt water poured in, causing the *Shin Fane* to sink rapidly to the bottom in six feet of water. There was a hissing and a big puff of steam as she settled on the sandy ocean floor. This probably stopped the fuel tank from exploding in the stern. All that was left above water was her burning wheelhouse.

Just about this time the Coast Guard rounded the headland under full speed. They set their siren howling when they saw the fire, but by this time the flames were beyond control. The great billowing plume of dirty smoke climbed high over the island beach, marking *Shin Fane*'s funeral pyre. Just the blackened hulk of her wheelhouse and deck structure showed above water. The tide was coming in and before long she would disappear below the surface.

The Coast Guard launched a Zodiac inflatable rescue boat and raced to the beach where we were all assembled. After they had determined that there were no souls aboard or lost, they began bundling all the kids and wives aboard their cutter. When I saw them coming I had an impulse to run and hide in the swamp and become a mad hermit like Ben Gunn in *Treasure Island*, never to be seen by human sailors again.

Our rescuers were a pleasant crew, and on the five-mile cruise back to our shore they shared a few nightmare stories with me of marine catastrophes they had witnessed—just to make me feel better. After I heard a few of their worst, I wondered why there is such a love of boats and life on the bounding main. The risks run high in the wild sea winds. There was a report to fill out on the way home and with that done Catherine invited the crew home once more to Windflower Downs for dinner. They kindly declined, saying that it must be a full moon for there were other calls coming in for assistance.

I had no insurance on the boat; after all, I reasoned, not a lot of money was tied up in the humble fishing boat. It was not the financial loss that bothered me, it was the physical and emotional loss of my good old boat. I had spent many days alone out in the deep waters on the *Shin Fane*, and it seemed as if I had got close to some *personality* that lived in the old boat, not just the wood and ropes and bronze fittings. I have never felt that way about a car or any other object, but a boat has a soul that cannot be replaced.

As the darkness crept over St. Andrew's Point, we said good-bye to our guests and tucked our tired little sailor into his bed. Alone I made my way down to the shore and stared out to sea. I could just pick out some black smoke over Boughten Island. I sat down among the coarse seaside grass and let my mind sail back over all the rivers and lakes and seas where my brave little flotilla of boats had ventured.

All the rafts and rowboats, the dory, the dingy and the curragh; the sailboats of every size and description. I had loved and hated them all. When I sail over the years in my mind, other boats present themselves that were a part of my life for a short time. With all my musical travels around the world I was able to find sailors who were willing to share their vessels with me. Sometimes I rented sailboats and only once in a while did my old jinx cause some disturbance on the waves. I owned a Friendship sloop for a short time, found it to be a most congenial boat and apart from the usual frustrations of sail, we had a great summer sailing around the beautiful south coast of Ireland from Kinsale. There was another beaching on the sands of Ballycastle. This time I was just a passenger on a fine old cruiser, *Ramore Queen*. The steering broke coming into Ballycastle harbor and the waves carried us up on the beach. The steel hull saved us from major damage, and we got her towed off the next day.

The *Shin Fane* had given me more trouble than most, but now a rush of sadness and loss swamped me for a while, not just for the old boat but for the end of the whole Island adventure. I knew that we would pull away soon, for our days of living on Prince Edward Island were drawing to a close. My first son James, born at St. Andrew's Point, is an Islander at heart. He loves the sea and a piece of the Maritime tradition is in his blood. He used to put on his little rubber boots and life vest as soon as he saw me heading down to the shore. I would smile at his mother's concern. "I want to teach him about sailing, and we need to get him a sailing dingy to learn the art," I would tell my wife quite profoundly.

"Perhaps you might consider enrolling both of you in a sailing, navigation, and safe boating course as soon as possible!" would come her not unkind reply.

With the sale of the house, Windflower Downs would now occupy a special place in our life's memories. We were leaving a lot of dear friends behind but Catherine found the solitude difficult with a baby to raise and the short summers were over before they began. With gloom I would watch the fishermen hauling out their boats in late September, covering everything with orange tarps—boats, traps, and all. Even the foundations of houses would be banked with seaweed and plastic to keep out the storms. These Island folk will tell you that summer is over by the end of Old Home Week—that was the last weekend of August! And it was true; you could feel a chill in the evening winds as the harvest moon grew in the sky.

Nevertheless, the leaving was going to be painful.

A late October rain made my teeth chatter as we climbed the iron stairway to the overheated cafeteria on the Wood Island's ferry. In a few weeks the Northumberland Strait would be frozen solid and this small ferry would spend the winter in dry dock. Then all the souls who lived on this eastern end of the Island would have to travel through the bitter weather all the way to the west to board the Borden boat with its ice-breaking hull.

Catherine is a child of the West Coast, and I think her heart was still attached to those snow-capped peaks and tall trees, and most of all to her family, particularly her only sister. But as we watched the red sandy shoreline disappear into the mists that covered the Island she cried openly. Tears for old friends and beloved fields and seashores and for that old house where we spent so many good times.

Five years later when I went back alone to visit the old place, I found one of our James's toy cars lying rusted in the grass. That one little car tugged at my heart and I could feel the mist in my eye for grand old times that slip away too fast. We have never forgotten our years on Prince Edward Island and all the fine times far outweigh the ones that left a shadow.

THIRTEENTH VERSE

Islands west and the captain's ghost

*F*or a year or more we searched for our next safe
harbor. We turned our mind to a western island and
took another, milder, ferry ride across the Georgia
Strait from Tsawwassen, British Columbia, to Vancouver
Island. The blizzards may have been raging on the eastern
shore of P.E.I. that February, but the flowers were blooming in
Victoria and people crowded the walkways around the
beautiful harbor. Tall ships rode at anchor and a young
accordionist busked beside a bronze statue of Captain Cook.
All along the sea wall were brass plaques inscribed with the
names of famous ships that had silently slipped in and out of
that fine harbor. This was my kind of winter environment!

We rented houses in Vancouver and journeyed back and
forward on the Tsawwassen ferry for some months always
looking for our next daydream. I suppose I am drawn to
islands and perhaps I am now on my westward run, for as the
years roll on I find I search for sunshine. I still dream of
tropical places and I still yearn for that ship that will carry me
to my heart's desire on some Hibiscus Coast. But Vancouver
Island was a fine landfall for our new safe harbor, and it was
there that our next sea place was waiting.

Again the fates took a hand in my journey. After being shown dozens of homes to the point of frustration, the ghost of an old sea captain invited us to share his space. His name was Captain Endicott Redvers Smith and he built a house on the Saanich Inlet in 1950 after he retired from a life at sea. We found his old, empty dwelling still unfinished and calling out for lots of care in 1986. Captain Smith had passed on a year earlier and the house had sat silent since then. It needed some major renovation, but its location was perfect for it nestled at the foot of a small mountain on a low cliff looking south into the sea and sun. The tiny ribbon of the Malahat highway could be seen on the distant mountainside. Nearby were the famous Butchart Gardens with their year-round blooms.

Best of all it had a beach and a boat moorage right below the house. The real estate dealings were very unsettling but we chased the dream and I do believe we were meant to share some life in that space. Then one late September day, when Catherine was full of our second baby boy, we moved into the captain's house.

Our peaceful moorage on Brentwood Bay

We had taken on another mountain of work. The walls were in poor condition and some rooms had no walls at all, only unfinished studs covered with cardboard to separate the rooms. We were struck by the awesome task of making it livable. "Look at these teak floors," I said with excitement, trying to brighten up the task ahead. "These are from a ship!"

"Look at the kitchen," moaned my wife. We sat down by the little bay, underneath the biggest arbutus tree I had ever seen, and we both knew, despite the work ahead, that this was the place to grow our babies.

On a tree by the driveway we found Redvers' old hand-painted sign that read "Ting Sang." We would discover later that this was the name of his home on the Yangtze River in China. There were many other discoveries that first month. James, who has inherited my art of plundering for old treasures, discovered a half-buried cedar dugout canoe in a large shell midden on the banks of the property. Then one day, when I went into my study I saw a beautiful brass signal pistol lying on my desk wrapped in a piece of navy cloth. James had been climbing in the roof space and found it tucked into one of the beams. He proudly presented it to me as a gift from one pirate to another.

I found out later that Captain Redvers Smith was a collector of nautical antiques and I like to believe he left this flare gun for me as a welcoming gift. There were still more discoveries to be made, for behind a row of his mahogany built-in bookcases, I discovered some old charts and handwritten ship's log entries as well as newspaper clippings that told some of his story.

He belonged to the Brethours—one of the early pioneer families to settle in the Saanich Peninsula and Sidney, British Columbia. One day I lit a fire in his stone fireplace, spread out the faded clippings and handwritten notes, and followed the captain's adventures in the almost forgotten era of the windjammer and the clipper trade to China.

He bought the land on Henderson Point, adjacent to the ancient Tsartlip reserve, in 1949. The site, he said, reminded him of the misty Chinese hillside landscapes along the Yangtze. He used the same blueprints for his Canadian home that he had used to build the one along that mighty Chinese river. The house was constructed in 1950, and Captain Redvers Smith retired from a life at sea to a place where he could watch the ships go by the Saanich Peninsula to the world.

The last piece of writing from Captain Smith was shown to me by his second wife, Viva. Written at age eighty-five, a few months before he faced his last great voyage, he wrote, "I'm not done yet, I'd still like to make another ocean passage under sail . . . just once more."

After a year or more living with the ghost of Redvers Smith, the old mariner captain, the house became our home. Another new baby was crying in the dead of night, and I walked him in Redvers' old study. Sometimes at four in the morning I found myself sleepwalking back and forward with a baby in my arms, singing a repetitive old sea song that I used to pacify all my children. "Mingulay" is a perfect rowing rhythm for rockin' the babies and it always works. I sometimes felt the presence of the old captain and it did not disturb me at all. I think he enjoyed the old songs.

> *Heel yer ho boys, let her go boys,*
> *Swing her helm round and all together.*
> *Heel yer ho boys, let her go boys.*
> *Sailing homeward to Mingulay.*

I was ashamed to be living in the house of such a respectable and experienced sea captain, when all I had to show for my years of nautical mayhem were a bunch of Marx

Brothers memories and an old wooden rowboat left behind in the sale. On a still evening, when I would row out into Brentwood Bay in his old wooden boat, I'd sometimes imagine he was sitting in the stern. He would whisper to me on the breeze, "Is this the best you can do, puddling around here in a dingy? What happened to all your sailing daydreams? Don't give up on them. Find yourself a real sailboat, and I'll come along to steer you right."

At first I ignored the whispers. Then it happened—that all-too-familiar tugging at my anchor chain. Sailing magazines started appearing by the bedside, and my car would not drive past the many marinas on the peninsula. I could be found loitering amid the long lines of sailboats, peering into portholes, and copying down phone numbers of vessels offered for sale on the back of my hand. People started to recognize me and invite me to visit their boats. Then, like the true addict that I was, I started to wear my sailing jacket and yellow sea boots. Dressed for action, I'd have an occasional beer at the marine bar. A certain envious squint narrowed my eyes when I watched all those barnacle scrapers and deck varnishers messin' about in their boats.

This time I was searching for the most traditional wooden boat I could find and that's how the American catboat hove into view. I became acquainted with these folky vessels in some of my musical excursions through New England. Year after year I played my music along that historic eastern coast from Portland, Maine, to Boston's south shore, and I tried to make a point of traveling the slow route down Highway 1 along the sea. I would leave the hotels at dawn to have the luxury of time to visit and to avoid the multi-lane traffic that would hurtle me past all the things that I felt America was really all about.

This probably explains one of the reasons why the rest of

the old band refused, for twenty years, to travel in the same car with me. (Well, they may be able to tell you other reasons, but that's their story!) They were always on a mission to reach their destination and get it over and done. I would have coffee in a clam shack as the fishermen were busy on the wharf. I would browse in wonderful chandler shops full of brass and rope and nautical maps in towns like Gloucester, New Bedford, Bath, and Camden. I often made a point of visiting the great marine museum at Mystic Seaport where the *Charles W. Morgan*, a fully rigged whaling ship, lies at anchor in the reconstructed harbor. The ship has been carefully restored to her mid-1800 whaling days shape, and the whole Yankee sailing tradition is finely displayed in this exciting museum.

It was here I first discovered the American catboat, and from the start there was something about them that drew me aboard. One of the Yankee sailors at the museum told me that everyone who owned a catboat had great affection for them. For more than a hundred years, they had a colorful history along the eastern United States. The original boats came from some European design and were used by fishermen to navigate up estuaries since they are mainly flat bottomed with a big centerboard and only about a three-foot draft. One big gaff-rigged mainsail, with the mast stepped as far forward as possible, moved them at a fine clip. At the turn of the century, catboat "sandbagger" races were popular along the coast of Massachusetts and Maine. I spent quite some time admiring the beautiful lines of these sturdy historic coastal vessels and later painted pleasant little pictures of them in oils on smooth board.

An article in *Wooden Boat* about the American catboat finally won me over. I propose that this magazine be banned! There should be a Surgeon General's warning pasted on the outside cover stating, "This magazine can be a hazard to those who are susceptible to sea fevers usually brought on by the sight of fine wood-worked boats." Then came mail-order books on the history of these sandbaggers. Now that expression should have struck a tiny alarm bell in me. It seems that in the old days catboat sailors would carry sandbags that could be shifted from one side to the other as the wind demanded.

One day I was hanging around the bustling yards at Canoe Cove, near the ferry terminal at Swartz Bay, when my next boat appeared. I had dropped into the marina sales office and talked to the salesman about his wares. "I don't suppose you've ever heard of a catboat?" I queried.

"You mean a catamaran?" he threw back at me.

"Nope, I mean a gaff-rigged American catboat."

To my amazement he reached to the window behind him and slid back the curtain. Then he pointed at the dock and sang, "Ta da!" And there, sitting bobbing at his dock, was a black-hulled "cat."

He had just received the boat in trade and, being a powerboat man himself, had no idea about its qualities or how to sail the thing. "But it's a beauty," he added honestly. It was indeed a beauty. It had been built in Port Hardy on Vancouver Island to a Hershoff design by Paul Miller. It was love at first sight of course. I could already see her sitting at anchor at Redvers' old buoy, and I felt sure the old captain would approve.

A sea trial was arranged for the following Monday. The salesman told me that he would have an experienced sailor take me out, a guy who had sailed three times across the Pacific and had raced every year in the Swiftsure sailing race around Vancouver Island.

I arrived at the dock at 11 a.m. on a sunny January morning, with a cool blustery breeze whipping up. The first salesman I had met had now been replaced by an experienced sailor salesman named Hans, who grasped my hand and crushed my knuckles with a hearty handshake. "Great day for a sale," he laughed, playing on the words as he had done, I'm sure, many times before. Hans was a tall fellow, tanned and rugged from a life on the briny deep and *Sylvester*, the twenty-two-foot catboat, was looking fine in the winter sunlight.

"If I buy her—" I started.

"And why not!" laughed Hans on cue.

"—I'll change her name to *Widdershins*," which is an old Celtic word that means something about going around in circles anti-clockwise. Yup! That's a good idea.

Hans pulled the green sail covers off the big mainmast and slid the hatchway open to the cabin. Everything was teak and mahogany and brass. The cabin was beautifully laid out with green velvet cushions, a small iron wood stove, and a compact little galley and head. "Surprising amount of space below decks," he said. "Forward bunks for kids, and your wife will love the galley. It was designed by a woman."

"Hmnnnnn," I said with a smile. "Maybe, yes indeed," I thought. "This is probably the boat for me."

A whole series of ropes were stretched across the roof of the cabin all neatly tied "Bristol fashion" around oak belaying pins. I followed the lines along the deck and let my eyes travel each one of them as they snaked their way to various parts of the gaffs, boom, and sails. The whole rigging, to my untrained eye, resembled a harp and we were about to play the fool's symphony. I felt a rush of instant gratification when the inboard engine started right away, sounding new and strong. I checked it out under the floorboards and it looked well cared for. Perfect!

We cast off *Sylvester*, and I was taken by her appearance. She was a beauty in every line, with her brightwork shining in the sun. We motored out past all the boat sheds and made our

Sylvester the catboat

way beyond the ferry terminal until we were just northeast of
Piers Island. A stiff little sou'easter was building up. I zipped
up my heavy woolen jacket against the chill and pointing to
the many lines strung across the deck, I asked Hans, he of the
vast store of knowledge, "What are all these ropes for?"

He answered me with a surprising, "Hey, I wish ya hadn't
asked me that question, pilgrim." (He was doing a poor John
Wayne impersonation.) "Shouldn't be any trouble to sail this
little sucker." He laughed. The trouble started, I think, when he
didn't release the mainsheet. It was pulled tight so that the
boom had nowhere to travel. He took all four lines that
hoisted the big main—throat halyard, peak halyard, topping
lift, and all—and gave them a mighty tug. The gaff went all the
way up and a great gust of wind smacked into it broadside.
Sylvester the catboat gave a shudder and promptly capsized.
The centerboard keel had not been lowered, the mainsheet
was fully tight, and right over she went. Now this was a heavy
twenty-two-foot boat! It wasn't a dingy out on a summer sail
in a warm lake. A boat like this is not meant to capsize.

It all seemed to be happening in slow motion. The mad

sailor, being a tall man, had clambered up on the side of the hull when we toppled over while I had grabbed the rail. Now I was stretched with my tiptoes barely touching the starboard rail grimly clutching onto the port with numb fingers. "Oh Christ!" I yelled. "We're going down!"

"No, no," said the big fella, quite unconvincingly, "this boat can't sink. Try to climb up here, where I am."

"Are you bloody well kidding?" I roared. "I can't move!"

The sail was now filling with icy water and the angle of the hull was changing. I was slowly sinking backwards into the water as the *Sylvester* was turning upside down. Sea water was pouring into the cabin through the open hatch. The lovely interior was becoming submerged. Hans was balancing up on the keel now as I was slipping under the ship. He yelled out frantically, "Ya gotta let go and get up here."

That familiar great dread of drowning was filling my entire being as water began filling my rubber boots. I truly thought that this time for sure I was a goner. Once again I was not wearing a life vest, and my heavy woolen coat was growing leaden with water so cold I knew I wouldn't last long. I pushed myself away from the catboat and floundered around her.

Among all my misadventures, this was the closest I have felt to that desperate numbing fear of death that takes your breath away and blurs the eyesight. I could barely keep my head above water and I was taking in gulps of the stuff. I thought about Catherine and our third new baby, due any day, that I might never see. Gripped in the terror of the moment I could almost see the newspaper article: "Man drowns on the day of his baby's birth."

I gave a frantic kick or two and grabbed onto the centerboard. Hans had forced it out to its full four feet and was now swinging on it. "Ya need to get on this!" he yelled. He pulled me up and the extra weight did the trick. To my absolute relief the *Sylvester* gave a jerk, and slowly the big mast rose back up out of the water. A miracle! "Oh thank the Lord," I moaned.

Hans, once again, being a tall man, was able to nimbly scramble into the cockpit just as the catboat was righting herself. Where was I? you might wonder. Well, when she started to come up I let go the keel and watched in dread as the heavy hull toppled back toward me. Now I don't know what angel was with me that day. Perhaps it was old Captain Redvers himself. I slid back into the water off the keel, pushed myself away, and was now under the starboard rail, which was too high for me to get a grip to hoist myself aboard. There was nothing to hold on to. I felt my face sinking beneath the weight of the woolen jacket and loaded boots as I tried my damnedest to keep my head above water. My lungs were bursting with the exertion of trying to stay afloat, and I knew I was getting weaker by the second.

I reached a desperate arm out toward Hans who leaned down and, with a superhuman tug, lifted me right out of the water raking my chest bone across the rail and landing me like a half-drowned seal into the boat. I was frozen and completely out of breath. I lay gasping on the deck for a few minutes feeling like my chest was caved in and shaking with the shock. When I had recovered, I grabbed a blanket that had escaped a soaking and huddled into it. "At least," I thought ruefully to myself, "I have survived one more bout in my joust with Neptune." The inside of the boat was floating in four feet of water but the engine started right away. Another miracle.

As we motored back to the marina, a big rusty ketch flying American colors passed by. Three bearded sea travelers aboard waved to us and one of them saluted and yelled, "Nice boat!" Thank God they hadn't seen the amateur capsizing. With frozen fingers we waved back, pretending to be comrades in arms in the fraternity of the sea. It seemed to take forever on that frigid return to Canoe Cove, and as we entered the marina, Hans, my boat salesman and near killer, commented, "I guess we'll forget buying this boat, won't we!"

When I got home, still wet and half frozen, I rushed to the bathroom and turned on the tap to run a bath. Catherine laughed so hard I was sure she would produce our next offspring there on the spot. Then she stopped and stared at me with horror when a most frightening thought struck her. "You're going to buy that boat, aren't you? I know it."

I sat shivering in the bath puzzling over the day's events. "There has to be a reason why that boat capsized. That boat was not meant to capsize! What caused that lovely little boat to capsize?" I mumbled half to myself.

"Hmnnnnnn, I have to find out. I'll learn about catboats— that's it! I'll find out why they're called sandbaggers. I'll discover why a lot of experienced old sailors have capsized them."

"Perhaps," said my always wise and honest partner, "you will also discover why anyone would want to own one."

The catboat pirates of Squally Reach

s Catherine had predicted, I did buy that sinkable "cat." After all, I'm the man who counts St. Jude of the hopeless cases as a friend. Oh, I suppose that if I had saved all the money I spent on trying to fix things up and make them float, I could be cruising the Pacific in one of Donald Trump's yachts. But just think how much fun I would have missed and how bored I would have been just

Setting out on a treasure hunt

languishing out there in perfect weather in a spanking new capital ship that never failed.

There is probably a little saltwater madness in one of Longfellow's poems, and now I feel qualified to quote his secret of the sea:

"Would'st thou," so the helmsman answered, "Learn the secret of the sea?
Only those who brave the dangers comprehend its mystery."

After that initial near-death capsizing of the *Sylvester* I decided to find out more about that mystery and learn the "ropes." The first few solo voyages were nerve-wracking, and I usually took a couple of reefs up in the sail before I ever went out. Later the wind became my partner, and I got the feel of the gaff and the wonderful way it all worked. After two months of sailing out there in the channel, where I almost lost my life, I started to feel that at last I had earned my seaman's stripes, and so one morning in May I set off in a "freshening breeze" (it felt more like a mini-gale) to sail from Sidney round the tip of the peninsula and south across Patricia Bay in the Saanich Inlet, past Senanus Island and home to my own buoy.

Heading round by Swartz Bay, I was daydreaming and watching Piers Island when a mighty blast from a departing ferry unnerved me enough to take in the sail and motor around the top of the peninsula. As soon as I had cleared the ferry traffic and the wind started to blow in earnest, I hoisted the big sail. Setting that gaff-rigged sail was a lot of manual work: first you haul up on the throat halyard, making sure that the peak doesn't fall down. Then when the throat is set, you haul up on the peak halyard until it reaches its limit. If you are in a bit of a blow, you need to be lively with the mainsheet, for the catboat, as I discovered, is not the most stable vessel.

The wind whistled up a blow of a squally twenty knots as I

started away from Deep Cove. Before long it started howling down the mountains, and I could feel that old tight-lipped fear grab me. I tried to bring down the gaff and take in another reef in the sail, but the wind was too strong for me to release the gaff. Now my starboard rail was almost awash, and not having any weight in the bottom I was sure I was in for one last sinking. I let out the mainsheet, and with the wind at my back it caught the boom and whipped it across, dipping into the water. I stood up just as the swinging boom came flying across, and it nearly took the old noggin off me. Amid the stars that danced in front of my eyes, I had a vision of a tall ship called the *Irish Rover*, and, just as in the song, she was turning round in circles, and finally, down she went like a stone! I shook my head and found it was me who had gone down like a stone. I was lying on the deck with a duck egg growing on the side of my skull.

I made it home safely to my pirate cove and after that there were many warm summer days exploring that sea mystery. I never did rename her *Widdershins* since nautical folklore dictates that ill luck will attend any vessel that has changed names, and I had the episode of *Shin Fane* to remind me. So for five happy years, with my catboat *Sylvester*, I plundered the "Spanish Main," although the modern maps call it the Saanich Inlet. From Willis Point to Tod Inlet, across to Bamberton and down the beautiful Squally Reach, the wild calls of my small pirate band echoed against the mountainside, and the eagles swooped down and answered the happy cries. My children became pirates the week the catboat arrived at our dock. Costumes were made and many a Treasure Island was explored. A little boy came up to me one day when I was picking Andrew up at school. "Are you a pirate?" he asked quite timidly.

"Arrah, me hearty, that I am!" I laughed as he bolted back

into school. From then on for the school year, Andrew's daddy was a pirate. I had to go to the school and tell the class a few pirate stories and get them singing some sea songs.

My little buccaneers never knew it, but early in the morning I would motor over to "Dead Man's Isle" and bury an old box full of sparkly things and cheap pearls from the treasure trove of the Sally Ann. There was a "real" pirate's map to follow, and it was the pride and joy of all the kids at school show and tell.

The Saanich Inlet is a magnificent body of water, where the ocean drops off to a depth of some eight hundred feet straight down from the steep sides of the Malahat slopes. A long fjord stretches down from Willis Point and ends in the famous salmon run at Goldstream. It is a fragile British Columbia treasure and long may it remain the domain of eagles, salmon, native dugouts, and small pirate vessels who might have to declare war on those few who want to plunder the quiet forest mountainside with bulldozers and blocks of little boxes.

On one of our voyages we discovered mysterious stone steps halfway down Squally Reach. They were part of an old

stone dock and first appeared as if they should belong to some grand house buried in the woods. When we tied up and explored the stairs we found that they climbed into

Andrew at four, my rambunctious second mate

the hillside and disappeared into thick underbrush. If they had ever led to a home it had now been swallowed by time. The children grew quiet as I led the crew on an expedition for treasure. They believed that Captain Kidd had erected the stairs for his castle, but that he had been caught and hanged in the Caribbean before he could make it back to Squally Reach in British Columbia. "But," as my little Andrew "Billy Bones" would comment, "we better look out. There are probably some of his buccaneers left hiding to guard his treasure."

Another adventure led to the discovery of the place that would become the children's favorite memory of their pirate days aboard the *Sylvester*. We had set sail one late afternoon from the strange stone stairs and started looking for our overnight moorage. After sailing a mile or so further along the reach, we edged toward the shore in the twilight. There we found a ruined boathouse and decided that here was the spot for our overnight adventure.

The sun was orange-gold on the tip of the west-facing slope while close to the cliff of the fjord we sailed into a warm dusk that was full of birdsong and perfumed pines. I was filling my small pirates' huge imaginations with tales from my own life as a pirate, when my first mate, "Billy Java," who on land was my nine-year-old son James, said with some excitement, "Dad, look! That must be Captain Kidd's castle." Everyone jumped up on the deck and stared in wonder as two old stone turrets appeared above the trees. I couldn't believe my eyes, but I seized the moment and acted as if this was the castle I had been looking for.

"Come on, my hearties," I cried. "We can see if the captain is home and maybe he'll let us stay for the night."

"I'm taking my sword," growled five-year-old Billy Bones. "He might make us walk the plank!"

"Why do we have to walk a plank?" whispered Clare, the youngest pirate, who was transformed into "Lizzie Bonny" aboard the catboat. "Can't we row our little boat to the beach?"

It was a magical evening as we made our way ashore in the small boat, much to Clare's relief. I led the raiding party and hacked our way with my machete through ten-foot-high brambles, up the old pathway that led to the castle. "Will there be live pirate skeltons up here like in Disneyland?" asked my little Lizzie Bonny, with some trepidation growing on her face.

"Don't worry," answered Billy Bones. "I'll blow their bones off with this real pistol." To my surprise he produced a small, hundred-year-old pistol and brandished it above his head in true warrior fashion. I didn't have the heart to take my old flintlock pistol off our heroic defender. He had removed it from my small collection of Irish antiques after I had told him this would be a dangerous voyage.

There was an archway covered in old grapevines, and we grabbed handfuls of the juicy, bittersweet fruit cooled in the evening air. Then we moved off cautiously and stopped at a stone bridge, just to make sure the "coast was clear." After all, I didn't want to land my sea raiders on top of some captain's wild party full of swashbuckling skeleton pirates. The stillness was so ghostly that every one of the crew spoke in whispers.

We climbed through the ruined house and the loneliness of the place struck me. I was intrigued that someone, quite a few years ago, had taken the trouble to haul all those stones up the mountainside and design a small castle complete with towers and archways. It sat in a spectacular setting that would have made any feudal baron proud. I watched the children fight their imaginary battles with Kidd and his cutthroats, and wished the original builder could have heard the happy play. I thought about the story told to me by local fishermen, who used the place to mark a good fishing spot. They said it had been built some time in the twenties by a wealthy man who had planned it as a retreat for himself and his wife. The poor man died the week the building was completed and his wife had never lived there. It had since fallen into its crumbling state after a fire.

There was a sadness about the deserted walls, and I sat there listening to my children's happy war and was full of my Irish childhood at Dunluce. I felt glad that they were building their own joyful life's memories around another stranger's unfulfilled dream.

After we were sure there were no evil captains or drunken skeletons lurking among the ruined rooms, we made our way back to our friendly cabin in *Sylvester*. I cooked a noisy pot of pork and beans and roasted spuds in a small campfire on the stony beach. As the little pirates drifted off into a starry night's dreaming, rocked by the wash of the tide along Squally Reach, Lizzie Bonny sat on my knee. With tired little eyes she stared into the sparkling heavens above the mountains and asked the most profound question of the whole day's adventure. "Daddy," she said through a yawn, "Are there elephants and pirate skeletons in outer space?"

Even though the children are a little older now, they still talk about the haunted Captain Kidd's castle and they still call Senanus Island in the Saanich Inlet "Treasure Island" or sometimes "Dead Man's Isle," and the cliff "Spy Glass Hill." Oh, I was full of the life, and with the Jolly Roger at the masthead and a crew of kids singing "Fifteen Men on a Dead Man's Chest" I was fulfilled. Finally I was the old captain of my own fine crew and first-class ship.

We sailed away the summer days of '94, and in the evening, when everyone was asleep, Catherine and I would sit outside in the calm evening breeze and watch the lights reflecting across the waters. One incredible night we heard a killer whale spouting and singing in the quiet waters of Brentwood Bay. I got to know the feel of the air on the turning of the tide, as a whiff of cool breeze ruffled the trees full of salty odors.

That breeze turned into a wind of change as the summer nights grew longer and an Indian summer turned our laneway to yellow-gold with fallen leaves from the big arbutus. We harvested buckets of ripe blackberries from the fields of our good friends the Towlers across the road. We drank summer wine with homemade bread and sang seaside songs as the sweet black pearl clusters were bubbling into Catherine's amazing jam. As the year ended and unsettled weather drove us deeper into more disturbed waters, those little jars of jam would remind us, with bittersweet memory, of that warm and happy pirate summer when all our hearts were glad.

CHORUS

All together now

I shared many wonderful times with our small growing
pirates aboard the catboat *Sylvester* while living at
Captain Redvers' house on the inlet. I grabbed as many
of those borrowed hours as I could when I was home and
gobbled them with joy. For the first time in all my years of
Irish Rover music I had no desire to head off for our annual fall
touring. There was no inspiration left in any of the members,
and I felt the stage show was getting stale. And worst of all, it
seemed that instead of being able to slow down after thirty
years, the tours were getting longer to feed the business
monster that successful music had created.

The house on the inlet was all I had ever dreamed about,
and I had hoped to keep it for a lifetime. But life is like a long
sea voyage, and you never know what weather lies ahead that
can cause you to alter your course. When those winds of
change blow across your bow all you can do is hoist anchor,
set your sails, and pray that your new course will carry you on
to a kindly harbor. Thank God I had such a strong sailing
partner in Catherine for both of us could feel a change coming
to disturb those peaceful summer daydreams. Something told
us to enjoy every day on that inlet with children who grow too

quickly, summers that end too fast, and old dreams that die a
sad death.

One day an old shipmate of mine called Billy Small, a man
with a giant soul who was "bread an' buttered" on my own
native shore, told me, "You've made a million people happy
with your music—now there's no joy left in your crew. I think it's
time to unload a lot of that burden and chase another dream,
let the *Irish Rover* steer on without you at the helm. Life's too
short to struggle to hold on to material things which have
become a heavy burden. There are no pockets in a shroud," he
laughed. "So get rid of this grand harbor and boat. Remember
your days when you were happy with an old rowboat and a leaky
caravan at Portrush."

I thought about Billy Small's words, and that year we
performed our Last Hurrah tour together. When the next drizzly
November came across the inlet, the pirates of Squally Reach
were blown off to another shore. Somehow we found it easier
on our emotions to part with the Ting Sang house than the old
property in P.E.I. We found another old house on yet another
beautiful country property on a small lake. This time there
would be no banks holding out their hungry hands every month.
Catherine loved it immediately, and so our promise to never
restore another old place was forgotten and away we went once
more. I imagined I could hear my mother laugh at the fact that I
was still following her gipsy style of shift and renew.

With recharged energy (I've never been one to dwell on
old aches) I went looking for a brand new band to set a new
music ship afloat. My new crew are top-notch Irish sailors and
the cream of the crop of Ireland's musicians, singers, and
storytellers. The music ship has taken on new sails and we have
completed two great tours Down Under and enjoyed the best
press in years.

Back home my three children continued to love the sea and

without any encouragement from me they have developed an attachment for old boats. I gave this affinity a bit of thought and decided the best I could do for them, in light of my own spectacular seafaring career, was to send them to sailing lessons. I also taught them the childhood poem that had helped start me on a life of unrequited love for the sea.

> I am fevered with the sunset,
> I am fretful with the bay,
> For the wander-thirst is on me
> And my soul is in Cathay.
>
> There's a schooner in the offing,
> With her topsails shot with fire,
> And my heart has gone aboard her
> For the Islands of Desire.
>
> I must forth again to-morrow!
> With the sunset I must be
> Hull down on the trail of rapture
> In the wonder of the sea.
> —"The Sea Gypsy," Richard Hovey

So now I write from a turn-of-the-century farmhouse on a small lake on Vancouver Island. The ocean is only two miles away over the hill, beyond our old barn, and there is an old sailboat lying in the long grass (probably beyond repair). Now we live surrounded by rolling green fields as I did in Ireland. There are hawthorn hedges in bloom and I am full of nostalgia for all that has passed and quivering with hope at what is in store. We have settled into this new life near Maple Bay in less of a rush to restore the house and with more concentration on making every day a good one for the family. I love the peaceful countryside and the early warmth of spring under the big oak tree where I can write my stories. The bushes are full of birdsong and the lake presents us with graceful swans and noisy flights of geese in the dawn. There are fewer tours and the financial rewards are not as great as before, but the most important thing to me now on this solo voyage is that at last I can choose my own speed. If the apples are ripe I can stay home and pick 'em. If the harbor is friendly I can remain a few nights longer.

One afternoon not long ago, I was sitting out on the dock by the Brig pub at Maple Bay, watching a young family arrive in a small sailboat. I could see they were coming up to the dock too fast and the boat rammed with a resounding whack. The young husband ran forward, jumping awkwardly to the dock holding his moorage line; unfortunately it was not attached to the boat. Then it tangled up around his feet and he tripped and fell heavily onto the floating dock. He picked himself up with the rope now wrapped around his legs.

The boat slowly drifted away and he put one leg on deck to stop it, while the other remained on the dock. He was now performing a crude splits routine as his wife jumped ashore. She casually tied the line to the dock and stalked off to have a cold beer in the Brig. The captain was trying to regain his composure as he followed after but not before he gave the little sailboat a hefty kick. He strode past me sporting a jaunty white commodore's cap with a gold embroidered anchor. Breaking into an affected sailor's rolling gait, he passed me and I gave him a knowing smile. He stared back at me with a wry grin of irritation and gave a shrug. I called after him, "Takes one to know one!"

Later in the pub I heard the same young captain talking to another boat owner. Gone was his insecurity. Now he was a full-fledged bar-side son of Neptune. Salt water was in his veins, and there was not much about sailing he didn't know. "And why not!" I thought, smiling a satisfied grin to the still waters below. Sails were reflecting the sunlight out there in the bay and I raised my glass in a toast. "It's true! There is nothing, absolutely nothing, half so much worth doing as simply messing about in boats."

I am boatless at the moment—happily I thought—but I had an experience recently that could change all that. I put together another music tour in the middle of these nautical confessions with my new show, Some Mad Irishmen. New Zealand and Australia was the destination Down Under. We left a Canadian winter day to land in a fine Kiwi summer and take that Celtic fun to most of the towns in New Zealand.

One evening near the end of the tour I sat with friends at a North Island harbor in sunny Whangarei. Ships from all over the world were moored there awaiting the end of the northern winter, and Canadian flags, American pennants, and some Union Jacks fluttered and snapped at the mastheads. Suddenly I knew I wanted to belong to this fraternity of the deep.

We took to drinking a couple of rum, and that's all it takes when you get a bit older, to bring out the song in the heart. We sang chanteys and planned exotic voyages. I waxed poetic that my last big dream was to sail in the sea lanes that Robert Louis Stevenson traveled in his yacht *Casco*. I seem to remember being very serious when I told them that I wanted to find his grave site—somewhere in Samoa at his property he called "Vailima" in the far South Pacific Ocean.

After the singing, the New Zealand sun painted the sky with a tropical paintbrush, then slid behind the hills of native bush. The little lights were starting to sparkle in the cabins of all the ships in the harbor. In the small galley kitchens, as evening meals were prepared, I heard the accents of the world mingle on the summer breeze with the sweet scent of flowering trees and cooking aromas. A great wave of loneliness came over me.

The song of my tin whistle carried across the water and I

longed to have Catherine and my three little pirates beside me. I gazed at all the ships and the traveling people and I wished that somehow I had been able to sail away with that little crew and follow the Southern Cross to make landfall in this distant harbor safe and sound.

I walked to my rooms as the evening came to a close and stopped to stare out onto the open sea. I heard a whisper come to me on the breeze sounding sweet and seductive and I think it said something like, "Build it and you can come!" So get ready, my dears, I am coming home with a head and a pocket full of plans for a new steel-hulled cutter. Big enough for us to live aboard for a year or more, perhaps down here where the sun first starts its run around the world.

It's said that if you stare at the last sliver of sinking sun on a clear tropical horizon, just as it disappears, you will see a most vivid emerald flash of light. They call it the green flash in Hawaii and if you catch a glimpse, it is supposed to bring good fortune. It can only be seen when the sky is cloudless and the ocean calm and untroubled.

Life is a journey that takes us through a lot of troubled seas, and I have crossed quite a few of them. I thank God I have also found my share of kindly shores and kinder people. There are many varieties of boats that can ferry us through the gale, so keep searching until you find a sound one and remember that there is always that hidden peaceful bay waiting at the end of the storm. When you find the entrance, sit back on your oars and savor the moment and keep your eyes on the horizon for the green flash.

These boats that carry us along the turbulent waterways of life are, I believe, all built for us before we start the journey. It's the way we chart the course, handle the sails, and maneuver the tiller that gets us to the dreamshores—if that's the desired destination. I am still building boats both real and imaginary, and it's a never-ending quest. Perhaps in my heart I don't really want to find that hopeful promised landfall. I have known too many people who reached what they thought was their island of desire aboard their perfect boat only to find that just under the coral sand of the final harbor there were jagged rocks trying to tear the bottom out of their boat.

These days I build a little more carefully, I watch the weather with a more seasoned weather eye, and I keep my hand on my own tiller. I hope that the moment before I am ready to pass on into the next and final ocean, I will catch a glimpse of that green flash as it lights up the idyllic harbor just as the tide pulls me out into the roar of one more foul-weather morning with the wind in my laughing face.

More classics of the sea from Whitecap Books

The Curve of Time
by M. Wylie Blanchet
ISBN 1-89509-926-9

Kayaking in Paradise
JOURNEYS FROM ALASKA THROUGH THE INSIDE PASSAGE
by Greg Rasmussen
ISBN 1-55110-633-7

Sailing Back in Time
A NOSTALGIC VOYAGE ON CANADA'S WEST COAST
by Maria Coffey
ISBN 1-55110-487-3

*Contact your local bookseller
for more information!*